CW00456951

West Country Medium

Published in 2011 by Antony Rowe Publishing
48–50 Birch Close
Eastbourne
East Sussex
BN23 6PE
arp@cpi-group.co.uk

A catalogue record for this book is available from the British Library

ISBN 978-1-907571-03-9

Printed and Bound in Great Britain by
CPI Antony Rowe, Chippenham and Eastbourne

West Country Medium

by

Maureen Scott

edited by
Terry Woodhouse

Front cover picture: an example of psychic art. The picture, which shows an astonishing true likeness to a younger Maureen Scott, was painted by another medium who had never met her. The process of psychic art is described in a later chapter.

Notes

I first met Maureen Scott through a golfing colleague who had been for a spiritual reading. He was most impressed at the things she was able to tell him, and found comfort in her messages following the loss of his wife.

When Maureen discovered I was a journalist, she raced upstairs and came down with an armful of foolscap paper. "I started to write my life story a few years ago, and every now and again I get a bit more down – all messages received through Automatic Writing – then it goes into the cupboard again," she explained. "I have been waiting for a journalist to come into my life to help me with this manuscript. I just knew one would come into my life one day."

She asked if I would take a look and, after talking to her at length, I admit I was intrigued – first of all by the nature of what she called her "work", which is acting as a medium for messages from the spirit world, and as a healer; and secondly by this Automatic Writing claim.

I'm not exactly one of the world's great believers, although I like to think I keep an open mind on subjects that we know so little about. And I have always fancied ghost-writing someone's autobiography, for as a sports journalist and business writer I have always dealt with facts rather than fiction, and never been interested in novels (neither reading nor writing them).

Maureen would be the first to admit her manuscript would hardly have gained a pass mark from an English teacher, but she is a good talker and has a wealth of interesting stories to tell from her experience of life and spiritual work. I took up the challenge.

All the stories in the book are Maureen's, related during a series of interviews carried out over several months, although one or two names have been changed to protect client confidentiality. I have carried out some research and used the Queen's English to the best of my ability to put the stories into some semblance of order and make the completed work an enjoyable and enlightening read. I hope I have succeeded.

TERRY WOODHOUSE

Acknowledgements

I would like to thank Terry Woodhouse for helping me to make this book a reality, because without his expertise it would not have been possible.

Also thanks to Myvanwy Jones, a medium I knew years ago who has since passed to the spirit world. When I was much younger she inspired me to do my work.

Heartfelt thanks also to my friend Joy Jelfs of Leicester, because she always had faith in me and cheered me on.

MAUREEN SCOTT

Contents

1 – My First Experiences

"It's a small world, don't you think? It's a small world." I was talking to a woman to whom I had just given a spiritual reading, and was seeing her to the door.

"It's a small world," I kept repeating, "it's a small world." I was getting embarrassed at this point, because I didn't know why these words were coming out. "Do you know what I am talking about, because I don't have a clue," I said.

The woman and her sister looked at each other in disbelief. and then went on to tell me the story of her family's trip to Disneyland in Florida. Apparently the holiday was one of the final outings of her sick young son, who died shortly after visiting the Disney park – which has an animated section about children and dolls called "It's a Small World".

Having never been to Disneyland at that time, there is no way I would have known that. The three of us all held on to each other, and there were a few tears.

It is just one example of many unusual scenarios I have experienced during my work as a medium – thankfully not all as emotional as that one, which was in fact just about the saddest reading I have ever given.

How did I become a medium? I am often asked that, and I'll tell you, it wasn't my choice! And my flight towards mediumship wasn't without its tears and tantrums. Something happened to me in the course of overcoming some personal tragedies and health problems.

My eldest brother Roy took sick. He smoked and smoked and, needless to say, suffered heart problems that affected his circulation. He agreed to a heart by-pass operation at the age of 63, but passed away on the operating table.

Losing my brother was so sad, because it was the first link to be lost in the family chain. I felt quite bereft, and thought everything that could go wrong with my life had now happened. But in a strange way it made me feel stronger. I started to have more positive thoughts – after all, I had come through all the sadness of also losing my mother and father, as well as my own little girl, and survived.

I was especially sad at losing my father, Tom, because he was my best friend and confidant. When he passed away the bottom fell out of my world; he was a man full of philosophy for life, and I used to sit for hours and listen to him. He was someone to whom I could impart all my troubles, and when he departed I felt a dreadful sense of loss and a void I just could not fill. When they took him away to the Chapel of Rest I just couldn't look, it was so painful. I just kept staring out of the window; it was like looking at a haze.

One of the strange things about him was that he never owned a toothbrush – all he ever did was clean his teeth by rubbing salt on his finger; but when he died at the age of 79 he still had every tooth in his head except one. And the only time he ever saw a doctor was when he suffered a painful bout of gout. I was just a little girl at the time, but I remember the doctor giving him an injection; then he went the colour of alabaster and collapsed; we all thought he was dead. Fortunately he recovered, but he would never again allow a doctor into the house! And I must say that attitude has rubbed off on me, because I never go to a doctor unless I am absolutely forced to, and in fact would rather visit a herbalist. The ironic thing is, however, that my son qualified as a doctor; he has a string of letters after his name and now specialises in psychiatry. But he is still a healer in my eyes – a gift, I was told by another medium, that he inherited from my side of the family.

Although I got on reasonably well with my mother, Winifred, it was my father who listened to all my troubles. We both soon learned not to talk about politics, because we would always have to beg to differ, but my father was a very earthy person. When he passed away I knew I had to pull up my socks, so to speak, and be strong. I had never been religious in any way, shape or form, but I found the strength from somewhere. I think we are all given an inner strength to get us through our trials and tribulations.

My dad made me promise to look after my mother after he had gone, and of course I did my best, but mum never really got over her loss. She was a very house-proud lady who would never allow a speck of dust on the carpet or a dirty dish to be seen in the kitchen, but after dad's passing she changed and went into a quick decline.

She said: "I have had a good life, although things have not always been easy, but now I want to join your father." I said: "I understand, mum, but it's not your time yet."

Gradually I began to feel better, and eventually felt quite proud that I had won the battle, or so I thought. But something else was happening to me – it was a very slow process that took years of inner searching and learning. That something else was spiritualism, although I didn't realise it at the time.

The first psychic experience I can remember was when I was 11 years old and I was playing with the other kids in our street. We used to use a derelict house, just three doors down from our home, as a kind of den, and one day I wandered up into a bedroom and had my first spiritual vision. By the window I saw an image of Mr Hill, the old man who used to live there and had died. I didn't know what was happening, I was so scared I just flew down the stairs about six at a time, ran home and was so out of breath that it took a while to tell my mum what had happened. I finally managed to blurt out that I had seen Mr Hill, but she said calmly: "Don't worry about it, he's not going to hurt you." You see, although she didn't practise as a medium, my mum believed in the spirit world and held no fears about it.

Some time shortly after that my mum asked me to run to the corner shop for some bread. I usually thought nothing of these trips, but on this particular occasion it was getting dark and for some reason one of the houses on the opposite side of the road gave me an eerie feeling. I didn't want to go past it. The next morning I couldn't understand why my mum kept the curtains closed, but she explained that the man living opposite, Mr Bernard, had died in the night and in those days neighbours used to keep their curtains drawn until after the funeral as a mark of respect. Obviously I had picked up some signal the previous night that all was not well in that house, and that was why I didn't want to walk past it.

I know I inherited my spiritual Gift from my maternal grandmother, Ada, although I didn't get the chance to really know her – I was only six years old when she died. I also know that several other members of the family practised healing, but it was herbalism they were into rather than any form of a spiritual nature; nobody was involved in orthodox medicine, as far as I am aware. I was always being sent down the road on errands when I was a small child, and often it was to the local herbalist for their preparations; I can still remember all the different smells when you entered the shop.

I heard many stories about how my gran used to work as a medium in a double act with my uncle, Fred Davis, who did the healing. I never really knew him either, but I'm told he was a really powerful healer and could literally knock people off their feet without touching them; according to the tales I heard, it was as if they had been hit by a massive electric shock!

But I don't think anyone else in the family has ever been very interested in the spiritual side of things, although one sister – who was very "anti" in the past – suddenly started to ring me up after her father-in-law died and one or two strange happenings occurred. Apparently the father-in-law had bought a television for his grandson to use in his own bedroom, and it worked perfectly until the night of his death, when it began to make unusual crackling noises. The grandson (my nephew in fact) also sensed his grandfather's presence in the room and the whole family became disturbed – which was weird because, as I have said, until then none of them had ever shown any signs of being interested in the spiritual world.

"Can you have a word with Mike," she said, and naturally I did. My take on it was that the grandfather was just saying his last goodbye. I told him: "Because you were very special to him, and he bought the set for you, that was the obvious way to make contact. You should feel privileged."

When I was young I heard stories about how my mother and her sister secretly slipped out to attend spiritualist meetings, because going to séances in those days was something you didn't talk about. It was all kept under the carpet – even my father didn't know at the time where they were going.

The subject was really taboo and kept behind closed doors, whereas today there is a much more open attitude and spiritualism is often discussed on TV and radio programmes. You have people like John Edward (*Crossing Over*), Derek Acorah (*Most Haunted*) and Colin Fry on Living TV programmes, all highly respected mediums in the public eye; there is the BBC-2 drama series simply entitled *Medium* in which the well-known American, Allison Dubois, acts as consultant, and on another digital channel there is the paranormal drama *Ghost Whisperer* inspired by the work of medium Melinda Gordon and on which the top-drawer American spiritualist James Van Praagh is a producer. Other people who have huge followings are Tony Stockwell (*Street Psychic*), Keith Charles, who has been known to help the police with certain cases, and Sally Morgan with her celebrity readings. And there seems to have been a plethora of films lately featuring paranormal activity, following on from Cate Blanchett as a psychic detective in *The Gift* a few years ago to the 2009 offering simply entitled *Paranormal Activity*, which purports to show some weird true-life filmed scenes that have had many adults jumping out of their seats in fright.

I'm not saying you should hang on every word of these programmes and films as if they are gospel, in fact some of them make me feel distinctly uncomfortable. I believe some of the mediums now involved in TV programmes are letting their egos get a little too big, losing the plot a little and not being good role models for the profession. And I think mediums who get involved in programmes with people like Derren Brown who, let's face it is a magician and illusionist, are more than a little unwise and doing a dis-service to serious clairvoyants and spiritualists.

The main point I am trying to make is that people are no longer scared of talking about the subject in public, wondering why we are here and what we are doing. In fact I have been to many meetings and conferences in London and other places where it is par for the course to have a medium on the panel. But go back 50 years and that wasn't the case. Nowadays I give lectures and teach about the subject – it's a completely different world where people are full of questions.

I didn't have a clue about all that when I first became curious about psychic affairs, but I will always be grateful to the first healers I encountered. I didn't know it at the time, but the spirit was priming me to use me as a communicator and healer. All the little things that had happened to me, and the things I had been told by mediums, they all started to make sense; it was like the pieces of a jigsaw coming together.

I made a lot of new friends and felt calm and at one with the world. Many times I put my feelings on the back burner, but something would always happen to renew them. Sometimes it was a remark from another medium, and sometimes it was people turning up at my door because they had heard about me from the spiritualist church. I realised later that it was some divine force egging me on.

The practice of giving readings started one Sunday morning when an elderly couple knocked on my door and asked for my help. I said: "I don't do things like that," but they insisted because of the stories they had heard about me. It transpired they had lost a young grand-daughter – and she came through to me in a flash! I could see this beautiful little girl, aged about six with Shirley Temple-style curly hair. I could hardly believe what was happening, but the old gentleman said: "Don't you ever give up your gift. You have to work at it." That was the first experience that showed me how important my work could be with the spirit world. From then on I began to visit spiritualist churches and attend psychic fairs and various meetings where I could meet like-minded people. My life was changing dramatically.

2 – Growing Up in Bristol

THE HOUSE

A house stood on a hill
looking very grand,
Built amongst the hills
on a small plot of land.

The flower borders up to the door,
the neat little curtains, the tiny windows,
Who could ask for more?
The little cat sat on the lawn,the goldfish in the pond.

The apple trees stood at the bottom of the garden,
bearing fruit for all to see.
Yes my friends, this little house
makes for a very happy family.

I never had a career. What time did I have to carve out a career – I was married at 16 and nine months (not pregnant, I hasten to add), and had my first child when I was nearly 18. That was 13 months after the wedding, just long enough to be decent, as my mother politely pointed out. She had begged me to wait a while, but of course I thought I was in love and knew it all. In reality I was just a little slip of a girl, but nevertheless we had a nice white wedding with all the trimmings. I remember the vicar saying he had never married two people quite so young, and needed a letter from my parents giving permission for the ceremony.

One of my claims to fame is that I was the youngest person to be married in that church, my local parish church in the Brislington district of Bristol – which has since been demolished, unfortunately. When we went to the vicarage for the rehearsal, the vicar was in bed with flu and gave us our instructions from his sick bed, holding a sinus stick up his nose, dressed in a white cricket sweater and almost hidden by piles of books, diaries and old stuffed animals.

The scene just had me in stitches – I had to excuse myself and find the loo to stop myself from laughing out loud; even after all these years I still laugh when I think about that scenario.

The marriage lasted 17 years, although I knew quite early on I had made a dreadful mistake. But I stayed until the three children were old enough to find their own feet, then I divorced him. It was my own fault that I hadn't listened to my parents or anyone else when I was a girl, but I did feel I had missed out on my teenage years – let that be a lesson to other youngsters who think they know it all! I didn't blame anyone for my plight but myself, so I had to bite the bullet and get on with life.

The only job I remember doing for a short while was working part-time at Woolworths on their Fancy Goods counter; I absolutely loved it. It's very sad that famous names like that are now disappearing from the high street.

My sister Pat was the closest to me when I was young. I was the baby of the family, the youngest of nine, and Pat was just three years older so naturally we had a lot in common. We were always going out together as kids and were also about the same size, so were always pinching each other's clothes and shoes. I was always a bit of a daddy's girl, although I'm sad to say I don't have many happy childhood memories. All I mainly remember is everyone falling out with everyone else, although as a teenager I managed to break out into the big world with Pat and we used to go jiving and get into a bit of mischief.

My parents were strict time-keepers, and if my sister and I were not home on time, Mum would be waiting at the bottom of our road to give us a right ticking-off. I know it sounds terribly sad that I don't have many happy memories as a youngster, but that's the way it was. I think if you are a member of a small family unit there are events to mark certain occasions that stay with you as happy memories for life, but that didn't seem to happen to me in a family of 11, although obviously the unit was never quite that large because when I was a child some of the older brothers and sisters had already got married and left home.

I really don't know how my Mum coped with bringing up nine children. There wasn't much money to spare in those days, and it was the time of tin baths and washing clothes with a mangle – youngsters wouldn't know what they are! Times were a lot tougher back then and I don't know how she did it, but we were all turned out immaculately, no hand-me-down clothes for us.

The household was also swelled most of the time by two or three pets. We had a massive tortoise whose shell used to get well polished by Dad, who wrote its name Oscar in boot polish on its back so all the neighbourhood knew where to return it to when it wandered off. Then there was a dog named Andy, a wild poodle that the window cleaner was scared of. It was vicious; I remember it cornering one of my brothers one day and then biting my Dad on the hand when he tried to deal with the situation. They had to call in someone from the local kennels to get it out from behind the settee, but when dad said it had to go I was so upset I ran away from home. I must have been about nine years old at the time, and apparently I was gone for a few hours – and when I did return Andy had disappeared. I was told it had gone to the kennels, and I never found out until about 15 years later that it had got run over by a bus.

The other childhood memories I have of animals involve the chickens my dad used to keep in the garden – and sell to his mates in the pub at Christmas – and the fur that used to hit me on the head when I went into the darkened shed to get my dried-out swimming costume. It was usually a rabbit that was being hung before becoming part of the family menu.

We always had parties on birthdays, but one of my most memorable parties was not as a child but as a young mother – when I told my daughter she could bring her little friends home to tea on her birthday. I got a shock when she turned up with the whole class!

My dad loved Christmas and made sure we had as many of the trimmings as he could afford, including a real pine tree every year. Pat and I, who shared a bedroom, were always the first up in the middle of the night to see what presents had been left. I remember the first doll I had that made a crying noise when it was turned over – we made so much noise with it that Mum came into the bedroom and took it away until the morning, along with all the other presents.

Not that our presents were a surprise – and it had nothing to do with any spiritual feelings. The truth is we used to ransack the house the week before Christmas looking for bags of goodies because we couldn't wait for the big day. One year we got found out because the large wardrobe in Mum's bedroom, which we hauled out to find the treasure, was too heavy to push back into its original place. More trouble ensued, but it was all part of the fun of Christmas.

Another time I was in big trouble was when I lost my young nephew Mike, and what I would have given for a bit of heavenly help that day! I was in charge of a small band of kids to see a cartoon film. However, on return to our house a head count revealed that one child was missing – my older brother's young son! We couldn't find him anywhere, and when we went back to the cinema it was locked and bolted; but we got the owner to open it up and a search revealed him fast asleep on the toilet floor, quite unaware of the panic and fuss that had gone on. What a relief, but it took a few years to live that one down.

My love of dancing goes right back to my school days, when we had regular dance nights organised by the School Club. I remember on one occasion Pat was grounded because she was late home the previous week, but so keen was she on meeting her hot date that we devised a plan that involved smuggling her clothes into the garden shed and sliding down the drainpipe outside our bedroom window. The trouble was she stayed out all night, World War Three broke out in the morning and we were both then grounded for several weeks!

Although me and my friends all lived in streets that looked like Coronation Street, my sister did bring a bit of glamour to the area when her date turned out to be Dave Prowse, a body-builder who went on to become an actor and play the Darth Vader character in Star Wars as well as the Green Cross Code man. Pat, aged about 16 or 17 at the time, would flounce out of the house in her head-scarf, tight skirt and sunglasses, and jump into Dave's bright red sports car. There weren't many cars like that around our district, so you can imagine a few curtains would be twitching. I think Pat thought she was a film star herself.

My father was a train driver on the old steam locomotives for almost the whole of his working life, and he loved the job. He used to tell me about the times during the War when certain bridges were bombed and he had to leave the train where it was and walk home in the middle of the night.

Although he could drive a train, he never did learn how to drive a car. But he lived his life doing what he could for his nine children – not an easy task in the so-called bad old days. The only time I ever saw him cry was when he had to go for a medical at about the age of 50; it was discovered he was colour blind and this led to him being demoted from his beloved engine driver status and reduced to shunting trains in and out of yards and sidings. The decision seemed to break his spirit; it was a heavy blow that I don't think he ever got over.

My mum had an extremely hard life. I can still picture her in the Anderson air-raid shelter in the back garden, but we weren't any worse off than any other working-class families. Besides raising the family, she also did her bit to bring in an income, and her claim to fame was that she worked as an usherette in nearly every cinema in Bristol. One of the bonuses of the job was that she got two free passes a week – but you can imagine the fight for tickets between nine children! Needless to say, there was many a good scrap between my brothers for one ticket, while my sisters and I were trying to stake our claim for the second pass. Luckily I was usually looked after by my older siblings and so saw quite a lot of the city's "flea-pits", as some of them were called. However, it all went belly-up the night we hatched a plan to get us all in. My sister and I went in with the free passes, but then tried to let in the rest of the clan by the exit door when we thought no-one was watching. Unfortunately we got caught, our parents were called and another World War broke out; somehow the pictures night out lost its magic after that.

My brothers were also very protective of me at school, so I suppose I led something of a charmed life as the "baby" of the family, which my mum continued to call me even after I was married; I never could cure her of the habit. But I must say this about my mum – she was quick to stand up for us if she thought we were being badly treated or had suffered any injustice. I can see her now bounding down to the school carrying a large umbrella, which must have put a bit of fear into the staff. I still remember the day one teacher locked herself in the broom cupboard when mum was on the warpath!

However, I didn't enjoy school, in fact I hated it. I played truant a lot of the time, although much of the treatment I received may have been the result of my sister's reputation, because I entered school three years after her – and she was always a bit of a handful. My sight wasn't very good when I was young and I had to have operations on both eyes, but that didn't stop the sewing teacher from singling me out and bullying me. In the end I just didn't go to her lessons. You always remember the teachers that treated you badly, don't you, and I still have bad memories of that particular woman.

I wasn't very sporty either, apart from swimming. I was down the local pool nearly every night – my swimming costume never had time to dry out properly.

When childhood was over it suddenly hit me – I had to live in the real world, which was quite a wake-up call after being sheltered from many of life's horrors. I was probably about 14 before I started to discover the opposite sex, but I had one major problem to overcome before joining my friends who gathered in the local park at 6 o'clock in the evenings. The big snag was that I was designated to do the washing up after tea, and this couldn't be done until my brothers had finished eating – which seemed to take an age some nights, with reading the daily newspaper being part of the meal-time ritual. I hovered like a praying mantis, then whipped up everything from the table and completed my washing duties before dashing out to the park.

I couldn't wait to leave school and join this adult world that we teenagers talked about so much. My mum would rebuke me and say that schooldays were the best days of your life – well, they might have been for her, but I hated them. On the final day of my last term some of the girls were busy saying goodbye to their favourite teachers, but I was too busy hanging out the flags and thinking thank God that part of my life is over.

If only I had known what was in store for me! When I got married and had children of my own I was floundering about in the dark somewhat; I kept thinking, how did Mum raise such a large family and still keep her head above water? I remember her stories about having to collect up the smallest children when the sirens went off during the War, and being forced to walk a considerable distance to some underground caves on the outskirts of Bristol that were used as shelters. "How did you cope?" I often asked her, and she would just reply: "It's a mother's love for her children." It was many moons later, after suffering some adversity in my own life, that I fully understood how she felt.

Some time in middle-age my Mum suffered a breakdown along with a bad attack of shingles, and was sent to Bournemouth to convalesce. She was only gone for a month, but it seemed like an eternity to me and was a real black spot in my life. When she returned she brought me a present of a wooden pencil box full of pencils and pens plus a rubber and sharpener – I never let it out of my sight for ages, and it remained my pride and joy for years.

Fortunately, as my neighbours continually confirmed, my children all turned out to be a credit to me, which was a great source of satisfaction. And of course I vowed I would never make the same mistakes again. But what did I do – I met another man two years later, thought I was head over heels in love again, and headed into marriage number two. That lasted eight years until I found out about an affair with a married woman from his place of work; it lasted just three months, but he moved out and I wouldn't have him back.

So it was back to a single life again, but I did feel betrayed and my health suffered for some time. The two marriage breakdowns had absolutely devastated me and took their toll; I stayed in a kind of wilderness for a while after losing the love of my life. I went through so many emotions and feelings of despair, and I must admit that for a time I couldn't see a way through; but there comes a point when you just have to change your way of thinking and get your act together if you are to survive.

I know I have blossomed like a flower, and have since become a very strong person in my own right, still close to my three children who have provided four lovely grandchildren between them. I am proud of the fact that I fought, conquered and won the battle, and having developed as a spiritualist and medium I have spent many years since those days helping other people to come to terms with their adversities.

3 – Finding a Spiritual Path

The very first time I attended a spiritualist meeting, I was so scared that I sat at the back of the church, hiding behind a pillar and ready for a quick exit. In fact I very nearly never made it because the traffic was so bad, and I am one of those people who won't go into an event once it has started. As it happened, I just made it in time, but I certainly wasn't prepared for what happened next. The medium, a Welsh lady by the name of Myvanwy, pointed towards me and said: "It's no good you hiding behind that pillar, God can still see you. And I know you very nearly didn't make it here on time tonight." I was blown away, but she added: "Come up and see me when the meeting ends."

I was all for dashing out the door at the end, but the man who had been handing out hymn books persuaded me to go and talk to the medium. Several people were gathered in an upstairs room for a cup of tea and a cake, but I was again trying to be inconspicuous in a corner when the medium approached me. She gave me a small piece of paper with a map on it. "Tuesday evening, be there," she said.

Initially I had no intention of going, but I suppose some sort of intrigue got the better of me eventually. It turned out to be a development circle for mediums in the Belmont Road spiritualist church in Bristol, and it proved to be an amazing experience. Myvanwy said: "Do you know how to meditate?" I said, "Well, I think so." She said, "Just meditate and tell us what you see."

We sat in a circle and I saw horses, but they weren't racehorses, they were Shire horses, those big, heavy working horses. And I kept hearing the word "York". I wasn't very old and I couldn't make head nor tail of it. I was on my way home when it dawned on me – put the two words together and it becomes "Yorkshire".

At the following week's meeting I asked if the word "Yorkshire" meant anything to anybody, and the lady next to me said: "That's where I'm from." That was the very first thing I ever picked up on, but of course I have since learned much better how to piece the messages together so that they make sense. That was my first little test from the spirits, who normally use a mixture of pictures and symbols to get their messages across – the medium has to learn to interpret these. Sometimes it does seem complicated and I'll send the thought back: "I don't get that." And down comes another symbol or word. It is all about knowing how to communicate with the spirits and passing on the right messages.

At that early church meeting Myvanwy told me: "You have got a lot of wisdom and knowledge. You will write four books, and one of them will turn out to be quite controversial." Of course, I didn't believe her at the time, but since then I have been doing quite a lot of writing. Myvanwy has passed over now, but I had the highest regard for her – the only medium I have ever met that I would really take my hat off to. I now know that first meeting led me to meet the people I was supposed to meet, and to read the books I was supposed to read. I didn't realise it at the time, but Steve the healer and Myvanwy the medium were the two people who were really instrumental in putting me on my pathway.

At about that time I visited another spiritualist church in Bristol and bumped into an aunt I hadn't seen for years. The medium came up to me and said: "You should be standing where I'm standing; you can do what I do." I didn't know what to make of it, but my aunt then told me about my grandmother's history as a medium, and the fact that my mother had always had an interest in the spirit world.

A true medium is born with The Gift, I know that now. But when I went to see my first medium on a one-to-one basis I warned my friend: "If she comes out riding on a broomstick with a black cat under her arm, I'm off!" As I have said, Myvanwy turned out to be a lovely lady who said that one day I would be doing what she was doing, and indeed would be able to give her a reading. She said in April that year something nice would happen to me, but I wasn't convinced. Like many people on their first visit to a medium, I just thought she was saying something to cheer me up.

But by April I had got the meditation bug. I sat in the healing room, very calm – and promptly had an out-of-body experience! I hasten to add it frightened the life out of me. I wasn't very old and I don't think I was ready for it. The trouble was I wasn't listening to the spirit world, so it grabbed me and sat me down and ... boy, did

I listen after that! It changed my whole outlook, and that was when I started to take my Gift seriously.

On that first occasion I was told: "If you see anything, don't deny what you see." And I saw my Mum coming towards me. It was as if I was in a toboggan on a ski run, with everything flying past me at speed. And although a lot of psychic people say they see things in colour, such as green fields and flowers, all I could see was white. At the bottom of the hill I saw my mother waiting for me, who had joined the spirit world by that time, and the overriding feeling I had was that I wanted to stay with her and didn't want to come back to this world. "Is this what death is like?" I kept asking my Mum, but she was saying to me: "You have got to go back; you can't stay." I felt as if a force was pushing me back.

When I came to, it was as if I had been delivered back by one of those old-fashioned message tubes that used to run on some kind of curtain track on the ceilings of large stores when we were young. It was such a weird feeling. I think I came back too quickly, and sat in a chair, hyper-ventilating. My daughter-in-law, who was with me at the time, became very worried and thought I was having a heart attack.

One of the mediums said: "Have you just had a funny experience?" That was putting it mildly! She added: "We knew you had, because the room kept going from light to dark, light and then dark again." When I got home I still felt very queer, and telephoned one of the mediums and said: "You are going to have to counsel me through this. I don't know where I have been, and I don't understand what I've seen."

"You should feel very privileged," the medium said, but I just didn't know what to make of it. I thought, "This is a privilege I can do without." However, it did change my whole life. Now, years later, I do accept that something wonderful happened that day; I just wasn't ready for it at the time. Since then I have had some wonderful experiences that no-one can ever take away from me, and I have seen many things I did not think possible.

I wouldn't say an out-of-body experience is a regular occurrence, but it is something that has happened to me quite a few times since. Now, of course, I understand more what is happening and I know how to deal with it. I just sort of coast off, usually to places I don't recognise. But nothing has ever upset me as much as that first experience.

It does all make sense to me now, and I suppose I have some natural gifts because I am mainly self-taught, but it has been a hard slog. It took me a long, long time to get to the point where I could trust the spirits and interpret their messages. I know there was a lot of testing going on in my younger days, and it used to drive me to distraction, but I know they now trust me as well. As I have said before, I didn't choose this way of life, I guess I just conceded defeat in the end and started to work on the gifts I have. Of course, I accept it is now my pathway; this is what I am.

The relationship with my mother has continued after her death. When I was young I didn't always like the way she treated my Dad; I thought she was a bit hard on him at times, and because he was such a lovely man I suppose that always rankled a bit. But just because you didn't see eye to eye all the time with someone on the Earth plane, it doesn't mean their spirit will not come through to you. My mum has come through and worked with me as a spirit guide on many occasions.

Granny Ada is now one of my spirit guides, along with my father. I also know there are two other young members of my family with some special powers – a niece and a grand-daughter – and that I now have the knowledge to pass on and help them. It has taken me half a life-time to polish it up, so now I just hope I can help to perpetuate The Gift.

4 – The Learning Process

A KING

A king came to Earth to be amongst men.
He lived his life and went home again.
He went back to Heaven to play amongst the stars.
We must all take a look to see what we are doing
to this land of ours.

Life is a gift, precious and new,
given by God for me and for you.
Never cast a stone in rage
Because, my friends, life is one big stage.
It is God's eternal book,
So open the pages and take a look.

Not all mediums have the best of reputations, but just because we don't all work the same way and see things in the spirit world exactly the same, it doesn't mean the service is not a genuine one. Some may try too hard to please, but I'm not tarring everyone with the same brush. Believe me, there are many people out there doing some sterling work; it just means we all have different abilities.

Many mediums say they can actually see an aura glowing around a human being. I haven't been blessed with that vision all the time, but I do sometimes get a sense of a colour around people and am definitely drawn to certain people for no apparent reason other than a kind of sixth sense. Let me give you an example: after I had moved home and didn't know any of the new neighbours, for some reason I felt drawn to one particular house every time I passed it. Eventually I met the occupant and I said straightaway: "You are a medium, aren't you?" And of course I was right.

The famous American medium Edgar Cayce had this gift of being able to see an aura around people, and claimed he could immediately tell facets of people's health and personality by the colour of the aura. For instance, red meant energetic but nervous, while orange was lazy and yellow was healthy; grey indicated illness and white was what everyone should strive for – perfection.

One of the first times I was aware of this ethereal hue around a fellow human was in my early days of attending a spiritualist church; suddenly I stopped hearing the speaker's words and became totally mesmerised by a sort of haze around him which appeared to me to be a confetti-like stream of tin foil. It was an amazing sight for someone not used to seeing that kind of thing, and I couldn't wait to tell him at the conclusion of the meeting. He was a man full of humour and laughter. "Thank you, I know exactly what this means," he said, matter-of-factly. And still being more than slightly entranced by the experience, I didn't press him further; I thought that as long as he understood then I didn't have to know any more, I simply bowed to his knowledge. "You are a medium yourself, I know," he added, "because I have been drawn to you all night." He went on to tell me several things that were a great help to me – so I felt I had been given a great reward that evening.

That happened quite a few years ago, and I have since come to accept that seeing an aura around a person is part of the medium's Gift. In general I have to agree with Cayce – a muddy or khaki colour indicates an illness of some kind, while a golden hue denotes the top-of-the-range happy disposition. Personally, I like to see daffodils around people, because they represent a really high vibration. At a reading recently I saw my home carpet become covered by swaying daffodils, which meant that not only was my guide pointing towards my client's Welsh connections, but also that she had a top-of-the-shelf radiance. People like that act as a pick-me-up, and I could feel the positive vibes and energy for quite some time after she left.

Sometimes the electricity just vibrates between two people on the same wavelength, and one of the best examples of this happened to me just recently when a Taiwanese man came to see me. We had what I would describe as a normal reading, but afterwards he introduced me to his wife – who had been waiting in a car outside – and when we greeted each other I could absolutely feel the static. She was a beautiful lady, a Buddhist, and must have been quite a sensitive person. When she went I was left with such a positive energy, I felt like a battery that had been charged – that's the effect psychic people can sometimes have on each other!

Getting such a high-level response from another human being is not an everyday occurrence, I just wish it was. Wouldn't it be great if we could bottle whatever causes this energy, or have people like that around us 24/7.

It was listening to other mediums and talking to them that helped me to prepare for my work. The spirits first started to come through me at night, when I was barely out of me teens and had a young family, and to be honest I was quite scared.

When I suffered my family losses in quick succession I was really going through a rough time and needed to talk to someone. I began to talk to my mother in my head, and I gained a lot of comfort and love from doing this. However, I started to become very erratic, using a huge amount of nervous energy. I couldn't keep still – I would grab a duster and tin of polish and go through the house like a tornado. Needless to say, I had the cleanest house in the road. But I was still so restless.

When I told a friend she suggested I might benefit from seeing a healer. I wasn't keen on the idea, not being religious, but she persevered: "It can't do you any harm."

So I went, full of trepidation, a 22-year-old young mother, not knowing what it was all about. The first thing this healer, Steve, said to me was: "You see the spirit world, don't you?" I just burst into tears, because the spirits had been keeping me awake at night, making me so distraught.

He said he could see columns and columns of people lining up in front of me. I said, "I don't understand. What do they want me for?" He said: "Maureen, these are people you will help in your lifetime. They will come from John O'Groats to Lands End. You have an amazing gift, and once you stop fighting this gift, and work with it, you will feel more comfortable."

And I did – eventually, but it took quite a few years. As I sat in that healing sanctuary I felt very relaxed and before long began to see mauve spirals of colour, then bright greens. I thought it was my imagination running off at a tangent again. On the way home, when my friend asked me if I had seen anything, I expected her to burst out laughing. But she said: "That's nice. Some people don't see anything."

I could hardly wait for the next week's session to come around. Now I realise that is when I first became hooked on spiritualism. I liked the peace and the tranquil feeling I gained from the healing, and one thing led to another. Even to this day it gives me an inner peace.

When I was first learning, I used to get together with a few friends and we would sit and meditate then tell each other what we had picked up spiritually from the session. In one of my very first sessions I could clearly see a blue hot water bottle, with the neck spitting out hot water, and sensed it was a warning in some way. But remember I was quite young and self-conscious in those days; I probably would not have minded telling of visions of angels carrying out some heavenly tasks, but I really didn't want to tell everyone that I had seen a blue hot water bottle. But the message from my spirit guide was: "Go on, you must say what you see, you must give this information." So I did, rather sheepishly, and they all looked at me as if I had landed from another planet. "Thank you for making me look an idiot," I murmured to myself.

However, the following week one of the male members of the group turned up with red marks around his wrists. "You and your hot water bottle," he moaned, then he told me how he had been scalded by spitting boiling water while filling a hot water bottle – and it was blue! "I wouldn't have thought a macho man like you would be the hot water bottle type," I said. "No, it was for my mum, who had flu. I wasn't used to filling a bottle like her's and I got burned when the water spat out," he said.

I was naturally sorry he got injured, but I was secretly pleased that something from my first vision had come true. It was as if the spirits were saying: "Leave it to us because we have the insight," and after that I was certainly not so reluctant to come forward with what I had heard and seen in meditation.

It was difficult at first to distinguish my own thoughts from the spirit teachings, but with experience a young medium learns to trust her own judgement while travelling along the pathway of knowledge and wisdom. I used to get tested a lot by the spirits, and ended up very frustrated on many occasions; but now we ride in tandem and they know what to expect from me.

I have learned how to recognise the various symbols from my guides. For instance, they have different signals to tell me if a person is in the spirit world or on the earth plane, and other symbols – in the case of pets – to tell me what colour they are. I think the best way to describe what I see is to liken the images to the deaf-and-dumb language of hand signals – it's that form of communication that the medium usually sees.

All mediums have trouble at times replicating exact words and symbols – for instance, it is difficult to differentiate between the names Bryan and Ryan, especially when spoken quickly; then May and June may refer to calendar months or female Christian names; and a picture of a string of pearls may mean exactly that or it may be the girl's name Pearl. It's a bit like playing the old parlour game Give Us A Clue; and sometimes I have to ask the spirits to speak up, or draw a bit closer if the image isn't very clear. Several factors have to be exactly right for a communication to take place, and much of the time it is down to experience.

One day, during a reading for a female client called Mary, I kept being shown a diamond ring. "They keep telling me the man in your life will be a gem," was my interpretation, and I could hear the chink of glasses so I knew she would meet her partner-to-be at a social event rather than the workplace. A fortnight later she rang to say: "Maureen, you'll never believe this, but I've just met a lovely man who gave me his card at the end of the night. And when I got home guess what his name was on the card … Diamond!" We both burst out laughing, but I must admit I did chastise the spirits for leading me around the houses on that one.

Among the many facets of spiritualism that fascinate me is astral travelling, but these out-of-body experiences have been quite rare and not something I can do to order. It is something that happens spontaneously when the energy is right, and I don't have to be in a trance state for it to happen. I could just be lying in bed when the subconscious mind drifts away, gleans the knowledge it needs and drifts back.

The first time it happened to me I think it was the spirits teaching me a lesson, saying in effect we'll sit her down, show her this and that, make her think about it and realise she has the necessary gifts to become a medium. It was a learning curve, and I'm still on it.

5 – Preparing for a Reading

A CANDLE

A candle stood blowing in the wind,
what a sight to see.
Billowing, dancing up and down,
dancing with glee.

Light a candle, send a light up to your God,
this will not cost you the Earth,
send a prayer, a loving thought.
Spend time to pray,
think about why the candle was bought.
It was bought to herald the dawning
of a brand new day.

I know only too well why most people go to a medium – because I have been in that boat myself! Although the spirits constantly use me as a communicating channel with life on Earth, I have always visited other mediums from the time when I first became interested in psychic affairs.

I mentioned earlier how I lost my brother Roy, and also my sister Audrey, but both have come through to me from the spirit world – not only with direct messages to me, but also through other mediums. However, I do have one problem in that Roy was very much the double of his father, and so at times I have trouble differentiating between the two. Mostly the messages are not about anything specific, just full of support for the work I am doing and guidance for the future.

Just because I am a medium doesn't mean to say the links will be any better for me than they are for anyone else. I can't explain or force the issue – there have been periods when I receive several messages close together, then others when they all seem to dry up. Unfortunately the spirits do not bless us with their presence on demand; you cannot call out a name and have them jump into the room, that is not how it works. You sometimes have to be patient, but there have been times when I have been simply day-dreaming and Audrey will come through. Those moments are worth waiting for.

When people come to me for a reading they often think it is just a case of me making contact and passing on messages, and that it is easy. But it isn't. The mind has to be blank for the spirits to come through – this is where the art of meditation comes in to play; the process will not work if the mind is cluttered up with worries about that pile of ironing in the corner of the room, or what to cook for dinner. A medium has to stay calm and balanced to be able to focus properly, drawing on the experience of forging all the right links after having learnt about the energy fields.

I meditate before every reading – call in my spirit guides and those of the client. For healing work I put on a background tape of soothing music just to get people more relaxed. Because I only ask for a first name, not a surname or address, I have been asked: "How can I call up a client's guides when I don't know who the client is?" The answer is that the spirits know! All I do is link up with them.

My work is all to do with energy fields and, although a lot of it comes from the client, I am very often left quite drained after a reading. Just recently a young woman came to see me who had lost her mother, and she was in such a distressed and depressed state that the session for me was like having some teeth pulled out. The spirits find it difficult to link on a depressed energy, but cases like this do occur from time to time. When you talk to someone who is deeply depressed it is often hard to get any real sense out of him or her, so working with a person like that is doubly hard and can be really draining for me.

Being able to go into a self-induced trance is something I learned through meditation, but I think achieving a high level is, like mediumship itself, partly a gift. I had help from my spirit guides to attain the knowledge I now have, but I believe you need a certain psychic energy in your make-up and then you can add to it by learning the technique. You have to know when to stand back and let the spirits use you. It's a disciplined process, after which I remember some of the detail but not all of it; listening to a tape afterwards can be quite an eye-opener.

The only time I experience the deep trance state is within a group of mediums, and they are all watching for certain pointers. There is definitely more energy within a group of like-minded people, but it is a very tiring process. I usually awake with quite a thirst, too.

But just as I won't touch hypnotism, some mediums refuse to have anything to do with trances. They believe it is possession of the mind, whereas I know that the spirits are merely using my subconscious to pass on messages. I am not afraid of the self-trance state because I fully trust in the protection given by my spiritual gate-keeper.

A medium has to be careful of someone who just wants to dump his or her baggage on them. I know from experience, because I have had the odd case that I have had to stand back from. Some people can become obsessional, but a medium cannot afford to get too close to a single client, to let them get their hooks in too deeply. It may sound hard, but there are people who need to see a psychiatrist or a marriage guidance counsellor rather than a medium, and in those circumstances I just have to be polite and as diplomatic as possible.

If the subject matter is not too severe I do try and keep a cheerful atmosphere, and keep the conversations "frilly", but the spirits can sometimes be very blunt and make it clear they want the message passed on exactly as it is. From time to time they make me squirm, but that is the way spirits are – the same as when they were on the Earth plane, not suddenly transformed with wings and halos, which is how some people imagine them. It is when their personal idiosyncrasies are revealed – such as two sugars in a cup of tea at bedtime, a favourite meal or maybe a piece of clothing – that the best evidence is produced and the clients take the most comfort.

One lady still looked very apprehensive at the end of our reading. I could see she was quite shy and uncomfortable in taking a lead, so I said: "Is there something else you would like to ask, don't be afraid." She said the session had been comforting to her, but that she really wanted absolute proof that it was her husband who had come through – and let's face it, we all would like absolute proof! However, on this occasion the spirits came up trumps. I said to her husband, mentally: "You heard that conversation, she wants proof it is you." He then showed me a candle, dancing and flickering in the wind – a picture I passed on to the widow. I wondered what I had done when she burst into tears, but then she got up and hugged and kissed me. She explained: "My husband passed just three days before Lady Diana, and as they carried his casket down the church aisle I asked them to play Elton John's "Candle in the Wind". She went out the door as if she had found a pot of gold – mediumship at its best!

On the subject of candles, I do light a candle or two at my readings because I believe they help the spirits to come through. I do find it helps the energy to flow, and sometimes the candle flames will even jump up, spit and hiss.

I think it is a general belief that candles have a spiritual essence about them, and there is good reason for this. Why do you think many churches allow the public in to light a candle for loved ones that have departed? Besides the emotion, tradition and ceremony involved, there is a practical point in that the candle sends up a light with each thought. I may have been blessed with the gift of being able to receive messages from the spirits, but I'm still a human being, no different from anyone else who has lost a close relative and grieved, so I still go into a cathedral now and again to light a candle and send up a message to my mum and dad.

Many other mediums attest to the fact that candles are a great aid in attracting the spirits. I don't often light two, but on a certain occasion I did, and don't quite know why. I was expecting the mother from a family which has shown a lot of interest in spiritual matters over the years, with several members coming regularly for readings. However, one of the two candles refused to stay alight on this particular day. I kept re-lighting it and it kept going out, like a damp squib.

In came Freda with a supermarket carrier bag. "What do you think is inside," she said. I hadn't got a clue, but I must say I came over with a bout of the shivers and felt sick; whatever was in the bag was giving me a bad feeling. I started to concentrate and said: "It's a doll," and described down to the last detail what clothes and colours (red and navy blue) it was dressed in. I had given up on one candle, but the other one now started hissing and flickering.

Freda then told me the story of the doll. She said her daughter had it as a little girl, treated it as her "baby" – as little girls do – but became certain as she grew up that she would never have a child of her own while she still had the doll. Freda said she didn't want to pass it on to anyone else, or even give it to a charity shop in case some kind of bad luck was passed on, and asked me if I would destroy it for her. At that point the one remaining candle began to bother me, for it was now well and truly spitting and almost jumping up the wall – it was obvious a spirit was trying to tell me something, and the message seemed to be: Get rid of the doll.

Freda went home and left me with the doll which I could see, when it was unwrapped, was exactly in the clothes I had described. I seemed to be on auto pilot and could still hear the spirit world giving me instructions. I rushed out into the garden with the doll, went out to the dustbin and broke it into little pieces, then I even cut up the clothes. Such was the strong feeling that I didn't want anyone else to have even a small part of it, and the problematic candle was symbolic of the doll and had to go as well – that was the message I was getting.

Once inside the house I started to calm down, put on the kettle for a cup of tea and let the other candle continue to burn. As the kettle boiled the phone rang; it was Freda sounding very spooked out. Apparently as she walked into her kitchen the radio switched itself on. "Don't worry, it's just the spirit world telling you the doll had been destroyed," I said.

In the following couple of months there seemed to be several television programmes on the subject of objects being cursed, and many of them turned out to be dolls. Some of the testaments were very interesting, if not unsurprising. But the final twist to the story is that I heard about 18 months later that Freda's daughter had given birth to a baby daughter. Apparently the girl and her husband had tried for a baby for about eight years, but it wasn't until the doll was destroyed that their dream was fulfilled. Freda will never forget the evening we spent with the dud candle – and I know I never will.

Another powerful symbol is the shape of the pyramid. The famous pyramids of Egypt are still a mystery in many respects to top scientists and mathematicians, but whole books have been written not only about the possible practical uses of such a shape, but also on the power and energy produced. There are claims that a pyramid-shaped object can improve the taste of food and water, stimulate growth, help healing processes, aid sleep patterns and assist dream activity in the subconscious mind.

I cannot personally vouch for all the claims of the pyramid studies, but I do believe the shape commands some kind of special energy, and therefore respect, so for many years I have kept pyramid-shaped crystals in the home. The ancient Egyptians obviously knew something that has taken the rest of the world many hundreds of years to perhaps only partly discover, and I must admit that Egypt is one country I have yet to visit and is on my "to do" list.

Nearer my home there are the ancient sites of Stonehenge and Avebury, which many people swear have great healing powers. I know people who have gained strength from hugging a stone, and on one visit to the Avebury ring I definitely felt a warmth from one stone while others remained cold. Would it be easier to contact the spirits in such a location of history and mystery? I haven't any personal experiences to speak of, probably because all my energy goes into my current lifestyle of giving readings at home – which I'm most comfortable with – but I'm sure many people have.

6 – Time to Move On

MIDNIGHT HOUR

It came upon a midnight hour,
when all the spirits came out to play.
It came upon a midnight hour
to herald the dawning of a brand new day.

When I take fright and feel like flight,
I stop and look and listen.
And as I stop to look around
the whole world starts to glisten.

In the dawning of a brand new day
I know with love and prayers I can find my way.
Spirit will teach me all I have to know,
the spirit world will show me the right way to go.

I am beginning to see life through different eyes,
yes, the spirit world can work through trouble and strife,
it is wonderful what you receive as you go through life.

Mine is a pathway already mapped out,
I will trust in the spirit, I will cast out fear and doubt.

After the children grew up I turned to my childhood love of dancing. It started with ballet lessons and evolved into the latest jives; remember, this was the time of Rock and Roll. I worked as a dance teacher for several years and was very happy to be rocking and rolling instead of dallying with the spirits. In fact until a few years ago I was still dancing at 100 miles an hour with a regular partner – it has always been my way of re-charging the batteries, and even now I still enjoy dancing.

But I know the avenue I took towards being a medium is where I am meant to be, and at the moment it is more important to me than forming any personal relationships. I've been there and done that – got married twice, had three children. I'm not ruling everything out, and if I met a medium or healer who was "grounded" then I might change my mind. But with my commitments to the spiritual world I feel I can't really afford to have anyone in my life who is too needy. The reality is that when you have someone in your life like that, you will find it difficult to focus on the things that really matter to you, and you will feel drained. It holds you back from what you want out of life. I know it's often easier to say these things than to actually do them, but I would advise anyone to think twice about a relationship that is not evenly balanced.

I have already admitted that the early part of my life was quite a sad time for me, and it didn't get much better in my twenties and thirties, mainly due to the marriages that failed.

I just had to find a new direction after losing a child and suffering two broken marriages, losing both my parents and one brother in quite a short time, and then my pet Yorkshire terrier. I know many people will think I'm mad to bracket a dog with my family losses, but pet owners will understand how close you can become to a beloved animal, and how deep the loss can be felt. I was getting really bitter at times. "Thank you God, thank you very much," I would mutter in anger, and I don't suppose I'm the first person to do that when life seems to offer nothing but one dark cloud after another.

Nowadays I am more work focused and very happy to have found my role in life. I suppose it is only natural that I tend to draw people near me who are interested in the same things as me – mediumship, herbalism and healing. It is with like-minded people that I feel most comfortable.

As I have said before, I didn't really choose to be a medium but I have learned to go with the flow. I always enjoyed being around other people and being a good listener for their problems, and as it happens I seem to have the kind of face that attracts people who want to tell me all about their problems. A medium once told me that I was the type of person who, if stood at a bus stop, would be approached by someone who would start telling me their life story, warts and all. And of course it has happened just like that. I have often been on a bus when a stranger has sat next to me – when there were plenty of other empty seats – and started to tell me their troubles. "I enjoyed our chat and now feel so much better," they say when they get off.

I must admit it does make me feel good about myself when I can help other people by just acting as a listening post. I remember the very first day I discovered my favourite little park in Swindon, where a little old lady in a red coat made it her business to occupy the seat next to me, telling me how she had just had her chest X-rayed following a beating from her husband. Can you believe that? After telling me quite a chunk of her life history, she got up, smiled and said: "Thank you, I have really enjoyed our chat; you have helped me get my problems off my chest."

I was 43 when my dad died, and my mum died three years later. I decided too many things had started to go wrong for me at Bristol and maybe a move would provide a new start-up platform. With one of my daughters living in the Swindon area, that's where I decided to make my new home, despite the Wiltshire town having something of a joke reputation. Although that is partly unjustified, with its wonderful railway heritage and providing the starting blocks for such showbiz personalities as Diana Dors, Gilbert O'Sullivan and more recently Melinda Messenger and Billie Piper, I must say at first I missed the hustle and bustle of Bristol's city life, with its harbour atmosphere and an amazing array of museums and so on.

Swindon may be famous for its road islands, but I must admit that at first it felt a bit like a desert island compared to the more cosmopolitan city in which I grew up. But I made a conscious decision to make a clean break, cut out the "dead wood" from my life and move forward, so I wiped the slate clean and started again. Mind you, I didn't quite realise how difficult that would be, and there were quite a few times when I just sat down and thought: What do I do now? Help!

It's a scary time, wondering if you have made the right decision that only time would tell. But I looked forward to making new friends and meeting new ideas and philosophies head on. I must admit things got easier as I began to get to know the local churches, and met a lovely lady at one who made me feel very welcome. One of the churches gave me a really warm inner feeling so I joined its local healing group, and was also getting better known as a medium in my own right and meeting more people through my readings. That also helped me to empathise with people who have problems in life; I fully understood how many of these people were hurting because of the difficulties that life threw at them.

It is quite natural after a major upheaval to wonder if you have done the right thing. At first I couldn't concentrate with all the noise of the town's traffic, but then someone suggested a nearby park and I discovered a quiet spot beside a pond. It was a warm day, the bluebells were out, trees swaying in the breeze as if they were alive, the birds were singing, squirrels were scampering around and a large swan skidded across the pond, putting on quite a show to the people enjoying the atmosphere. A family of ducks were making a bit of a din while preening under one of the trees, their green heads reflecting like velvet in the sun; and a child's pebble thrown in the water made a large ripple that just reminded me of man's conscious thoughts. Then the various shades of green of the trees and grasses, along with the myriad of colours in the flower beds, just appeared as a tapestry – a bit like life itself. It made me feel quite spiritual. At that moment I received a message from my dad: "Will this do for you, girl?" I had to bite back the tears. "Oh, thank you. This will become my little piece of heaven; where better to find inspiration," I replied.

I didn't find the house move easy, and at first felt a little isolated, but I just knew in my heart of hearts that I was in a new town for a purpose – although I didn't quite know what that purpose was. I started to listen more to my helpers and spirit guides, and found a new kind of trust; I now felt as if someone was steering my ship on a charted course, with me as the captain, instead of continuing to be in a wilderness. I was listening to my own inner child, acting on my intuition, and it was a wonderful feeling. It probably appears a sad thing to say, but I was beginning to feel refreshed and happy to be alive for the first time in my life.

I was feeling lucky to have found my little bit of paradise almost on my doorstep, which I knew would be a great source of inspiration and would change the scheme of things for me. I always knew that if I trusted in the spirits it would all work a treat, and so it proved; they put me to the test again and I think I passed.

Life was now becoming a bit hectic, although like a true Gemini character I do have to keep busy and I do have a dual personality. I was trying to get used to my new surroundings, building up a clientele for psychic and healing readings, writing as much as I could and trying to fit in a social life; every time I attempted to take a rest, it all speeded up again. One medium said to me, "Your life seems like a vortex," and I could only agree.

Then I purposely slowed my life down after moving house; I needed time to balance my life again and focus on my mediumship and my writing. I did feel as if I needed a jolly good holiday to re-stock the energy flow, especially after a buyer-from-Hell experience in Bristol and the whole trauma of moving house. The place that came to mind was Spain. Come on spirit friends, weave your magic, I pleaded. So I went to a retreat that I had heard about, but unfortunately it didn't quite work out as successful as I had hoped. It didn't turn out to be the right crowd for me, and didn't completely invigorate me as I had hoped.

However, once back in Swindon the park continued to be my little piece of heaven, taking me out of the rat race and close to nature. With all the rushing around in the quest for material things I'm sure mankind generally has lost its way and would benefit from being more in tune with the planet and with what Mother Earth has to offer. For me, listening to the birds singing is one of the most pleasing sounds on the planet – and it's all free! It's also a fact that when the sun is shining people smile more and stop to talk to each other more often – it surely goes to prove my point further that Mother Nature does have an effect on all of us.

When I first moved to the Swindon area I rented a small room in a so-called alternative healing centre. I encamped alongside an aromatherapist, an acupuncturist, a reflexologist and someone working on the Alexander Technique which concentrates on body posture.

The very first client I had was a Sri Lankan gentleman, and being more than a little apprehensive on my first day, I watched him climb the stairs to my inner sanctum situated above some shops, and I could "see" a stethoscope hanging around his neck – what I mean is, although I couldn't see one in the physical sense,

I was somehow aware that one normally belonged there. "You're a doctor," I said, and he was stunned at this introduction. But he must have been impressed at the reading, for he not only told the receptionist on the way out how accurate the session had been, but he also promised to put my card up in his surgery. Not bad for starters, I thought.

But among the people who came to see me when I first moved to Swindon were one or two with an ulterior motive. They were other mediums who tried to keep up their guard and did not let on about their gifts, although thanks to my psychic ability I was able to quickly pick up the signs. I think they just wanted to see who I was and what I could do, and I can understand them wanting to find out more about a new kid on the block, so to speak. I suppose I was the same when I was first developing as a medium and keen to meet others with this gift. But the fact that I had some rough treatment from some mediums in my new surroundings left me with a slightly defensive attitude, resulting in me keeping them at arm's length if ever I came across them at psychic fairs and so on. It was my way of putting up some kind of shield for my own psyche.

It's like any other business – there's a certain amount of competitive spirit, if you will forgive the pun, and I am well aware that when one person starts to become well known there is bound to be envy from some quarters; they don't want you becoming more popular than them, which is human nature I suppose. But some people go too far – believe it or not, I even had a couple of anonymous warning phone calls, a bit of street life that you might think only happens in drug gang and Mafia films! "What are you doing here on our patch?" I was asked in pretty torrid terms. There was silence when I asked for a name, but I said: "Look, if you haven't got the courage of your convictions, don't ring me again." And when I started my business from this local alternative health centre, I had quite a few phantom bookings – people making appointments which they didn't keep just to waste my time, perhaps hoping I would get exasperated and move on. But I was going nowhere, and gradually they were the ones who got fed up and backed off.

I remember one medium I went to see years ago refused to give me a reading. She said: "You're a journalist. You've just come here to try and trip me up." I said: "I do try and write, but I'm not a journalist." However, she wouldn't believe me and things went downhill in that particular relationship from there on.

Whenever I have been to other mediums, usually in a spiritualist church, I find they nearly always have the same built-in intuition as me and immediately pick up on my work. "You work for the spirit world. You're a medium yourself," they say. And being connected to a church doesn't always stop the cattiness; I've seen people argue about who is going to make the tea! And there is a lot of basic information that some of them don't seem to be aware of. I tried to talk to one about transfiguration, and she said: "What's that?" And I'm not joking. Some mediums are not prepared to learn, they just seem content to stay on a certain level, and I've never been happy to do that.

Even at the Arthur Findlay College of Psychic Science in Essex, one of the biggest spiritual learning centres in Europe where I once paid a lot of money to attend a course because I was keen to learn and improve, I wasn't impressed by some of the things I witnessed. One lecturer was just reading from a book – how impressive is that supposed to be? And some of the other things I witnessed I didn't feel comfortable with. I suppose I had heard so much about this college, and spoken to so many people who regarded it very highly, that I just had to go and see for myself. The course I attended included Trance, Clairvoyance and Healing, but I think I probably left it a few years too long before enrolling, because by the time I went there I had already learned my trade pretty well. I think for aspiring mediums and people still trying to get their head around the whole subject, it would be a good learning curve, and it is certainly set in beautiful grounds near Stansted Airport. But my own experience left a lot to be desired – I spent a lot of the time giving messages to the tutors instead of them teaching me!

There are good, bad and indifferent examples in all professions, and mine is no different. Of all the mediums I have witnessed I think Stephen O'Brien is my favourite. He is principal of the Academy of Psychic & Spiritual Studies, which has its headquarters in Swansea, but is also a prolific writer on spiritual and paranormal topics. He claims to have been psychic since childhood and has been involved in television productions since the 1980s. I like him because he appears to be what I call "grounded" – he can command an audience, but has never forgotten his roots and has no airs and graces, dealing with each subject right from the heart. I saw him on stage in Bristol many years ago and was very impressed by both his manner and his results.

I suppose most times when I have consulted other mediums I just wanted some kind of confirmation about my own path, mainly to do with my writing. But now I have full confidence in the Automatic Writing that I have been receiving. I haven't spoken to another medium about it for a couple of years – I've moved on.

7 – Spirits or Ghosts?

It's a wonder I ever settled in the Swindon area after my first experience, because the very first room I used as a base had very negative vibes within it. One adjoining room normally used by an aromatherapist had a great welcoming smell about it, as one would assume, but the room allocated to me – usually occupied by an accupuncturist – was not so hospitable, and even some of my clients had an uneasy feeling, which wasn't good for business.

It felt cold, even on a summer's day, but I don't think it was anything to do with the fact that needles were generally stuck into people in that room – I haven't got anything against acupuncture, in fact my mother often went for sessions and came back feeling like a spring lamb. It's just that some rooms have a welcoming aura about them, and some have the opposite effect, although I suppose you have to be a bit psychic to pick up on these things.

Do ghosts exist? Of course they do – you cannot discount as a crank every single person who reckons they have seen one! I've seen a few in my time, but I have never felt threatened by them. Some mediums believe there is a kind of holding area between this Earth and the spirit world, and that is how ghosts are seen – that they are spiritual entities that have not wholly passed over. It more or less coincides with my viewpoint, for I believe the spirits are sent over to the "light" when they pass from this Earth, but sometimes they do not move on completely and appear to be on the same frequency as the humans left behind.

All I can say is that I have had messages from people quite soon after their Earthly deaths, so if they were in a between-states situation they certainly weren't there for very long.

The appearance of a spirit at the time of a death, or forewarning of a death, is an experience that many of my clients can relate to. What usually happens is that an individual will have a chance meeting with an old acquaintance, then learn that he actually died the previous week; or maybe the spirit puts in an appearance the night before he departs this world. It's a ghost story to the non-believers, but to me it's just the spirit saying its goodbyes.

One of my clients actually wrote the time in his diary of a "meeting" with a former colleague; later it was learned that the man had actually passed away at the date and time stated in the diary – but at a place miles away! So he had met the spirit saying its goodbye!

The subject of transfiguration is still a very controversial one, I know, with sceptics wanting photographic proof or film evidence before they become believers. What happens is quite a complicated business, with the spirits building up ectoplasm to manifest an image that can be seen by the human eye. Many people in the nursing profession, including a member of my family, have witnessed an energy force actually leaving a body after death. But often I can see a spirit actually coming out of a client during a reading – I have to look away and break the gaze because I don't want to scare the client. People have sometimes said to me, "Maureen, your face has changed. You look like a little girl." Going into a trance-like state to enable this to happen is something that requires a lot of experience. It's not something that happens all the time, but it has occurred on occasions when I have been talking about psychic matters, or people around me have been talking on the subject. When you get several mediums together, especially, there is a lot of power present.

My first encounter with this phenomenon was when I went to a small church one Sunday where a medium was at work, but the day did not start out as a good experience. To say I wasn't very impressed is putting it mildly – in fact I wanted to get up and run for the nearest door. No doubt she was having an off-day, as the vibrations were right down on the floor. The chairperson must have sensed this as well, because she said: "Come on now, someone speak, or laugh, or I will think you have all joined the spirit world." And it got worse as the meeting progressed.

However, a small girl sitting in the same row with her mother gave me a broad smile; she was wearing a bright orange jacket and had a lovely energy around her. I can't think how we struck up a conversation, but the session ended with me inviting them back for a coffee – and it turned out to be a wonderful evening.

The mother, who I knew had certain spiritual gifts (and now regularly gives Tarot readings in the West Country), held my ring and just let the spirits do the talking. And she was so accurate, answering so many things I felt I needed to know – such as whether moving to Swindon was the right move for me, did I have the skills to work as a medium and healer, and would I become an author in time to pass on the message to others.

Then she exclaimed "Wow" and the most marvellous trans-figuration took place – I had never seen anything like it. It was so powerful that I had to turn away, and I was afraid I might go into a trance and scare the daughter. I tried to keep abreast of the situation as this lady saw all my guides, and went on to describe my mum and dad in detail. As I continued to look at her I could see my parents so clearly, along with my brother, and could see the guides coming and going. It was the most amazing experience. When I had to avert my eyes, she understood completely. "I know how it feels, it is as if you have been staring at a light bulb," she said. "You have to get your focus back on board."

I suppose it's only natural that many people without faith need scientific evidence and remain sceptical of the forces that mediums believe produce these clear figures. The situation is not helped by the fact that most photographs and films purporting to be of spir-itual sightings – as with UFOs – are of a quality that even the rawest amateur could look at and realise they were charlatan efforts or hoaxes. Misty pictures of figures behind white sheets come to mind that make me cringe.

However, every now and again there are photographs devel-oped that survive the experts' scrutiny and are left in the "unex-plained" folder. Some scientists are continuing to try and prove that the brain and the mind are separate entities, and that the soul lives on after the body expires; one of the most respected authors in this field is George W Meek, an American who came over to Britain and visited many other countries to carry out experiments with mediums and whose books include *After we die, what then?* Retiring at the age of 60 from an engineering career, he then spent many years following in the footsteps of famous inventors such as Marconi and Edison in attempting to create a radio wave system that would transmit the voices of spirits. In fact he recorded hours of conversations in the 1970s and '80s – and produced photographs purporting to be of plasma and energy fields emanating from human bodies – that have been kept for posterity by the Foundation he organised. Some of the early recordings were a little difficult to understand on his "Spiricom" machine, but Meek admitted that the world's first inter-plane instruments were "a modest beginning" and that they were bound to be crude – to be filled with static and frustrating to operate. He did assume, however, that before too long more modern systems would evolve that would enable easy communication with the spirit world.

Then there was Britain's Sir William Crookes, one of the first scientists to study plasmas and radioactivity, who went on to closely examine many mediums at work and took a number of supporting photographs. He concluded their results could not all be put down to magic, and that they pointed to the possibility of an "outside intelligence".

How far has the psychic fraternity progressed, since the discoveries of Crookes, Meek and their like, in convincing the world at large that there is an after-life? Not very much, unfortunately. I do think it is amazing that in the 21st century, with all the modern technology available, no-one has yet produced clear-cut evidence, but maybe one day!

I can, however, relate a couple of my own experiences on the subject of spirits having an Earthly presence. The one occasion I bumped into one was when I was working in a healing room and could clearly see the image of a nun, a sister of mercy, standing close to the bed. When I went to move around the bed I felt something hit my shoulder. The bed was very close to the wall, but I know I didn't touch the wall – I just didn't get out of the way quick enough.

The other occasion was when my children were small and we went on a caravan holiday to Weymouth where, I still remember, the weather was absolutely awful. It was during the last evening that my husband sat bolt upright in the middle of the night, asking who touched him on the shoulder. It certainly wasn't me or the children, but the room felt very cold and we put on the light. We both had this eerie feeling as a shadow moved around the walls; neither of us slept a wink for the rest of the night, and in the morning we couldn't get out of there quick enough. I had this compelling feeling to leave, and even an offer by the park owner of an extra week because of the bad weather couldn't persuade me to return. Maybe someone had passed away there, for caravans and mobile homes can be haunted just as much as any bricks-and-mortar house. I was convinced there was a presence in that caravan that I wasn't sure about, and I wasn't going back to find out!

On the subject of spirits, Gordon Smith says they appear to him to have a pale golden light around them, but that's not how they show themselves to me. I see a cloud of steam as if it's coming out of a kettle, then an image appears; I only get an outline, but one thing that is often clear is the hair.

I always keep the spirits at arm's length because if they come too near I can feel them clashing with my own energy field. Their energy is different to ours, and it can cause a shock to the aura. I can sometimes feel them inching forward, maybe to show me a photograph or perhaps the image of a baby, and I have to send out the thought: "Whoa, my friend, go back!" If the spirit asks to come forward, then I can prepare for that; but I have to be disciplined in what I do and make certain they are aware of my golden rules.

I also need a few minutes to recover after a trance healing session. A medium needs time to realign, to straighten up, before anyone else can tap in to the force, otherwise the body can be in for a deep shock. Mediums have to be aware of the human boundaries and frailties as well as the spiritual ones.

As I have said, some people have remarked that my face actually changes when I have let a spirit through and I am relaying philo-sophical messages about our earth plane, and others have said my voice has changed, maybe dropped to a lower tone. I have actually witnessed this in other mediums – I have seen their faces change, making them look younger, and this is the result of the psychic energy building up.

But no-one has ever said my accent has changed, or I've been speaking in a foreign language. I know this has been the experience with some mediums, and I have witnessed things like this. But I've also been at meetings where the medium has started to talk in what seems a rather obvious false Irish accent, and I've just got up and left. Spirits don't work like that, not in my book.

Disregarding the possibly dubious aspect of mediumship, however, I have heard many trance-mediums speaking in various voices, although I haven't always been sure where those voices are coming from. Is it a spirit, or is it the subconscious mind of another person being picked up and making itself heard through the medium?

One of the most intriguing direct-voice mediums was Leslie Flint, who died in 1994 leaving behind a library of tapes recorded at his séances over 42 years. Although he never went into any sort of trance, voices could clearly be heard – many from well-known departed personalities including Winston Churchill and Rudolph Valentino – but many doubting testers failed to come up with an Earthly explanation. I have also heard a tape from the well-known medium Colin Fry that really made me sit up. He claims to be able to channel voices when in a trance state, and on the tape I heard – as he was singing in a Judy Garland voice – it would be hard to distinguish him from the genuine article. He can be heard to say: "Are you ready? Shall I start singing now?" That tape blew me away, but on the other hand one or two of the examples I heard at the revered spiritual college at Stansted left me less than convinced.

So are these voices from the Other Side or from some down-to-Earth impressionist with a sense of humour? There are good and bad in every walk of life, but it is a medically recognised fact that some people suffer from schizophrenia and even multi-personality disorders. For instance, I knew of one woman who spoke in the voice of a normal 25-year-old for part of the day, then reverted to that of a meek and mild middle-aged person another time, and later on could sound like a mad 65-year-old wanting to bash everyone she came into contact with. She had all these different personalities going on in one body.

My son is a psychiatrist, so I do know a little about the studies that are being carried out into people with these voices in their heads. Mediums don't always claim to know where the voices are coming from, but the spiritual world is opening up much more these days and we may discover a lot more in the near future. Already some members of the medical profession and some hospital wards are allowing hands-on healers as a supplement to their own diagnosis – something that definitely would not have been tolerated a few years ago.

Ghost busting is something most people are familiar with these days following several films and TV series on the subject, the latter usually involving some celebrities being stuck in a large house out in the wilds somewhere. There are mediums who specialise in this kind of work, but it's not something I get involved in very often, although occasionally I have been asked to visit a place where there have been abnormal sounds or sightings. To my mind they are not exorcisms, but rather what I term "rescue" work.

Recently I went with a small group to an old West Country boilerhouse where apparently no-one would venture because of "funny goings-on". My initial impression was that the building certainly did not have a welcoming feel, and from my first few steps I felt very cold. The room we were taken to didn't outwardly appear to hold any untoward secrets, but then we heard a cough – it definitely didn't come from our small group, in fact I can assure you it was not from anyone who was living. This made things more interesting as far as I was concerned, and I sharpened up my instincts. Then all of a sudden there was the sound of some object skimming across the floor.

When we emerged upstairs the group organiser asked about the kind of sound we had heard. His theory was that it was a marble being rolled across the floor, because the building had once been a children's hospital. Certainly the room had a strange feel about it, but I like to keep an open mind about these things. Strange things can happen, and do, it's just that we don't always understand the communications from the Other Side. But there had obviously been so many sad events in that building, including rumoured suicides, that the bad vibes were easily picked up. It's not a building I would want to go back to.

Normally on a ghost-bust the medium's job is to connect with any spirits present, tell them they don't live there any more and that they need to go over to the "light". It doesn't always work first time, and sometimes it can take several attempts, but I have been successful in sending spirits over when I have been invited to certain places.

I've never been asked to get involved in an exorcism that involves evil, and even if requested I never would. That's a bit deep, and my take on the subject is that a priest is better suited to sort out those problems. In fact I'm not attuned to the word "exorcism", I find it rather frightening. I've always tended to stick to the "light" – anything that strikes me as a little bit on the dark side, or I don't feel comfortable with, then I'll leave well alone. I know some mediums do meddle in these things, but it's not for me.

However, one of my experiences involved a woman who had miscarried during pregnancy; she asked me to go to her house where she had detected a presence. She had a new man in her life, but apparently he kept picking up vibes that he was not welcome in that house.

I must admit I was aware of something paranormal the minute I reached the door; there was a kind of force that was saying: "Don't come in." And I picked up very quickly that it was the spirit of the unborn child that was sending signals to the boyfriend. He said to me: "There is something that doesn't want me in this house; I could sense it as soon as I put the key in the door and started to walk down the hallway." I was glad he admitted his feelings, because I was struggling to tell him the truth as I could see it. I didn't want to embarrass him, but I had to agree that it was as if a kind of barrier had been erected in the hallway, making it difficult for him to pass.

My experience is that you have to talk to these spirits as if they are children. I sent up the message: "What you are doing is naughty; you shouldn't be doing this. You have to stop doing this and move on." And I was later informed that the activity stopped after a while.

All mediums have a gatekeeper or doorkeeper, because bad spirits can come through when you are open and off your guard. I use my father as doorkeeper; he stands by my side acting as a kind of sieve, watching for what I call the "playboy" or "rogue" spirits – they are the ones that are not what they pretend to be. We all know there have been people on this planet who are not very nice, and unfortunately they don't change in the spirit world and suddenly adopt a halo and wings; and you can also get naughty children.

But no-one should just open up to the spirit world willy nilly – that's why I wouldn't touch an Ouija board. Before every reading I call up my dad before I call up the client's guides. I wouldn't dream of opening up to just anyone, and if I get a funny feeling about something I don't go there. My father always warned me not to mess around with an Ouija board because he reckoned they were evil, and I never have done. Mind you, I do know some mediums who use them quite nonchalantly, but it's not a method for me. I have had people ask me to join them in an Ouija session, in fact quite recently one man I know showed me this board he had made, and it was a beautiful piece of work. But I told him straight I won't get involved in anything I don't feel right about, it's as simple as that.

I do know of one woman who became obsessed with the board, playing around with it on a daily basis, and although the messages started off quite light and airy, after some time she received the warning "I am going to kill you". Needless to say she ended up needing psychiatric help.

Anyway, I'm not convinced it is always spirits coming down; my belief is that it is often just a build-up of energy. But if people who are not mediums do get a spirit coming down and they don't know how to return it, there could be a problem. Remember, it's not just your Ant Sally or Uncle Jim who may come through!

I once went to a medium who turned out to be an Irish lady who had just come back from the Orkney Islands, but immediately I was in her presence I had a funny gut feeling. I told her: "If I said to you 'Get thee behind me Satan', would you know what I was talking about," and she said, "Oh yes." I said: "You have got into the dark side of this somehow, that is what I am picking up." She said: "You are right, and that's why I have come away from the Orkneys. I did get involved in a witches' coven there, but I wanted to get away from that."

Shades of *The Wicker Man* film starring Edward Woodward, maybe, but strange things still go on in some parts of the country. I went to this lady for a reading, but it turned out that I was doing most of the reading for her! I told her bluntly: "You have lost your mediumship. They have taken it away because of your involvement with the dark forces. Once you do that they will pull away." She said: "Will I get the Gift back again?" And I had to tell her "No. The spirit guides won't work with you any more."

I've read a lot about witches and seen TV documentaries about what they get up to, and I know it goes on all over the world – in fact they still practise human sacrifice in some remote parts. And you cannot write off Voodoo, which has been brought into the news headlines because of the Haiti earthquake disaster. This brand of spiritualism, taken to the Caribbean by African slaves and later mixed with bits of Catholicism and other beliefs, is still a way of life for the majority of the population. I am well aware that its some-what evil reputation is probably largely thanks to the exaggerated minds of the Hollywood film makers, but there is a certain amount of truth in past associations with animal and human sacrifice, and people sticking pins in effigies. If it has a whiff of black magic I won't have anything to do with it.

I'm not saying all witches are bad news, because I understand enough about the subject to realise that many pagan religions are merely following Mother Nature, celebrating the summer solstice and so on. But it is not all innocence, either. I'm sure some mediums have been asked to help people who have become mixed up in the "dark" side, but fortunately it has never happened to me. I have never wanted to touch into that side of spiritualism. No way!

A medium once said to me: "You are very guarded about your gifts," and when it comes to those kind of things I certainly am. I use my Gift to help people – the bereaved and those who need healing. That's it as far as I am concerned.

The experience of spirits interfering with electronic systems may come as a shock to many people, who probably feel these are the pure fantasy of Hollywood film-makers, but I can assure you it is a well-known phenomenon to mediums. Lights flashing on and off without the aid of a human hand; even televisions and radios coming on unexpectedly – while not being exactly everyday occur-rences, they are incidents that most mediums have learned to take in their stride.

There have been many recorded examples of tape and film machines suddenly having stopped working at crucial points, and parts of tapes having been found blank when replayed. Sylvia Browne tells the story of how, when she was writing one of her books, a chapter on The Dark Side was initially drowned out on tape by "weird screeching static", and a later session was continu-ally interrupted by the lights mysteriously being switched on and off.

For my part, "somebody" seemed to take a dislike to some of my writing matter for this book when it was being transferred to a computer, for some sections mysteriously deleted themselves on more than one occasion. I have also experienced examples of the spirits not liking the manner and content of certain readings with clients. It doesn't happen very often, but when it does occur I know the spirits are upset and getting their own message across loud and clear. It happened when a woman called Melony came to me for a reading and the subject matter turned to abuse; I just had to tell her that my conclusion was that the spirits did not want us to tape that particular conversation and had put the blocks on it. I had to concede defeat.

On another occasion my small tape recorder, which I have used for countless readings, simply refused to work at all once the session started, although it recorded my usual test message perfectly. My only conclusion that night was that "somebody" did not like the subject matter that was going to be discussed!

But it is a well-known fact to mediums that the spirit world loves to play around with our electrical gadgets to make their presence felt. One of the weirdest experiences of this kind happened to a friend of mind who was working as a postman; his route was mainly in the country and one day, while delivering a parcel to an elderly lady, he was called into the house to look at the television set. "The set is switched off, but take a look and tell me what you see," she said. My friend could see the outline of a man's face, and described it to the householder. She said: "That is my husband, who died recently. I have been seeing his face for some time now, but I wanted someone else's opinion just to prove I was not going mad." My friend – until then a sceptic of paranormal stories – searched around the wiring and confirmed the set was definitely switched off. I believe it was the husband's way of saying goodbye to his wife, telling her he was all right and was still around her.

Another common phenomenon is the appearance on audio tapes of noises that no-one detected in real time. And I don't believe it's a case of being out of range of the normal human hearing system, such as a high-pitched whine that only animals can pick up.

There are so many thousands of corroborated stories of this kind of happening, and one in which I became involved concerned a couple living in South Africa. Their daughter came to see me after losing her brother in a tragic accident; his spirit came through very quickly and I was able to pass on a lot of information that brought her comfort. She sent a tape of the reading to her parents, who were obviously impressed and came to see me some time later when they visited England.

I did a reading for them, and thought nothing more about it until the daughter contacted me and said there was something strange on the tape her parents had taken back to South Africa. She said: "When mum and dad got home and played your tape they were very surprised to hear some sort of crashing sound about halfway through; it was quite loud, drowning out your voice in one part. They brought in another family member, a nurse, who listened intently and told them, 'That is a heartbeat if ever I heard one – and I have been nursing for 30 years. I know a heartbeat when I hear one'."

The couple were moved and comforted by what they heard. But was this their son's heartbeat captured on tape? I'm afraid I don't have the answer, but I do know it is just one of many strange sounds that have been detected on recording tapes that are hard to explain. Case histories of recordings made in haunted buildings are littered with countless similar examples.

There is a film called *White Noise*, made by director Geoffrey Sax in 2005 and starring Michael Keaton, which is based on EVP (Electronic Voice Phenomena) and tells the story of a spirit talking and eventually making a visual appearance on tape, which the character was able to manifest thanks to computer technology. The story was fact-based insofar as there are people who spend their time searching the radio-waves for voices from The Other Side. In fact during my learning experiences I joined a group of mediums who attempted this – unfortunately with no success while I was taking part. But the main reason I found *White Noise* so fascinating is that it was a serious dramatisation of this phenomenon, with a man searching for messages from his murdered wife, and I would recommend it to anyone interested in this subject.

Besides creating noise, spirits can sometimes bring certain smells with them, such as the perfume they used to wear or the tobacco they smoked. One day I had a mother and daughter come to see me, but as soon as I linked with their father's spirit the whole house reeked of toast. It wasn't just me – we could all smell it. The daughter explained that her dad always made toast first thing every morning.

Another person was mystified by a strange smell in his bedroom after his mother died. It wasn't there all the time, but just seemed to be present intermittently. And unfortunately it wasn't a pleasant perfume-type aroma that some people have detected from relatives who have passed away. But I had previously been able to pass on – correctly, as it happened – the fact that Tony's mother had died of a cancer, and I am afraid it is not the first time I have come across this set of circumstances. It seems to be a fact that people who die of cancer can continue to emit a rather unpleasant odour; I can only assume that the spirit of Tony's mother wanted to stay in close contact with her son.

When a spirit is telling me that death was due to a heart attack, I feel a real thump in my heart. And at one reading recently I could see a gentleman who I knew was dying of cancer; I saw his glasses being removed and the sheet being pulled over his face. I was shocked when told he was only 52 years old, for in my vision he looked much older. Being a medium has its very sad moments.

8 – Visits from Madeleine

TO OUR DAUGHTER WITH LOVE

A box of chocolates for Christmas I did get.
I take off the lid and look inside,
Shall I have one, oh no, I might regret.
I might get fat, I might put on weight.

But I can hear good old Dad calling me
from his heavenly home,
Saying go on girl, you can tempt fate.
Alright then Dad, just one and no more.

I got stuck in and, oh dear, I forgot to count the score,
never mind Dad, I will try to do better next time.
Alright I will forgive you, daughter of mine,
but promise me this, you will make your life have
some reason or rhyme.

Because I am watching you in my heavenly home,
I am guiding you and loving you
So that you can reap that which you have sown.
Mum sends you all her love as we watch
our beloved daughter from up above.

Because, daughter, you are so spiritual and filled with love,
because in life you were our best friend
and me and Mother loved you until the very end.
God bless you Mum, God bless you Dad,
I can think of you now and not feel sad.

Some people do spend time and money in attempting to contact famous names from the past. Elvis Presley is an obvious favourite, and probably Michael Jackson as well now that he has passed over, along with prominent figures from the pages of history such as

Winston Churchill, Oliver Cromwell and Mary Queen of Scots. Thankfully that hasn't happened to me with clients, nor have I had any famous celebrities come through to me in readings.

But I have received messages from a little person whose name has been on the lips of just about everyone in the civilised world – and it's a name that has involved an international police investigation. That name is Madeleine McCann, the three-year-old Leicestershire girl who went missing in Portugal in May 2007 while on holiday with her family in the Algarve resort of Praia da Luz.

Normally I am in a light trance state when spiritual messages come through to me, having meditated in readiness for a reading to be conducted in a disciplined way. But I wasn't in a trance-like state when Madeleine first appeared, I was just winding down with a drink. It was one of those situations where I was sitting down for a rest, the mind not being preoccupied by anything in particular; but I think in those circumstances we are prone to day-dream – that is when spirits sometimes drop through without being called, although it is not the norm by any means.

For about a week I was aware of this small child standing near my bed, and naturally I began to ask questions about who she was. Having lost a child many years ago, a baby girl that was stillborn, my first reaction was that it was my own child's spirit trying to connect with me. She has come through to me in the past, sitting at my feet to give me energy and support, and also sometimes through other mediums, who have described the way she was dressed. And they got it spot on, because the outfit they described is just how I would have dressed her; it was how I brought up my other two girls – in a very girlie fashion complete with ribbons and bows, frilly socks and so on.

When the name "Madeleine" came through strongly to me, shortly after she went missing and while the hunt for her kidnappers was in its early stages, I wasn't seeking to contact her or become involved in the case in any way – as I will explain, getting mixed up in police proceedings is just not my style. It just happened that something from this little girl – call it telepathic messages if you like – began coming to my bedside over a period of about a week, and at first I didn't have a clue who she was.

The sceptics may say that the newspapers and newsreels were so full of her that she was bound to be in my head somewhere, but that isn't true. She wasn't playing on my mind and, as I have said, I didn't even realise who she was at first. The newspaper headlines I read all screamed "Maddie", and so – call me naïve if you like – I honestly didn't instantly associate the name Madeleine with the missing girl. I asked: "Where are you?" and she just kept taking me to Portugal, talking about water, showing me a deep well and repeating the name of one particular person.

The first time she appeared was shortly after I had finished a reading for a client, and I was still quite psyched up I suppose. I was sipping a cup of tea, trying to relax, when she came through and explained what had happened to her – and I was just reduced to tears by the vision that appeared to me. The feeling was so strong that I felt choked – it was simply dreadful, and I cannot bring myself to repeat the name she mentioned because it would be too distressing for all concerned. I just begged her not to come through to me again like that.

However, she did, and the next day I was watching television when it showed people releasing balloons on her birthday. I could hear my spirit guide saying: "It's no good you watching that, it's all hype." I had a very prickly feeling about the whole case.

Why would Madeleine come through to me? I don't know, that's the honest answer. But a medium did say to me many years ago: "You have a special affinity with children, that is why they will come through you," and I suppose it's true. Perhaps they think I will help them in some way, maybe to get justice on the Other Side.

Obviously the family are hoping that she is alive and will one day be found. I know Madeleine's heartbroken parents Kate and Gerry will never give up the search for their daughter or the people responsible for the kidnapping, and nor should they. However, my belief is that the person who was ill in prison and admitted to the kidnapping early on is a complete liar and just threw a red herring into the police case for his own publicity.

Three years on I don't know what is happening so far as the Portuguese police are concerned, although I am aware that official reports are still ongoing in England. But what I know about Madeleine would not be much help to the investigation. Firstly, the police would probably think I was just another nutty spiritualist with a barmy theory, and secondly there are so many thousands of wells and drainage shafts in that part of Portugal that it would be virtually impossible to check them all out. From the visions I received I believe she is around water, but I am pretty sure similar versions have already been forwarded to the police and the family by other mediums, so I would be adding nothing new to their files.

I have often wondered if mediums should get more involved with the police in helping to solve crimes. I know that even raising this subject is bound to invite a barrel-load of sneers from the cynics, but it is a fact that mediums and detectives do come together at times – and not always in the fictional TV programmes.

Only once did I submit some information to the police, and that was quite a long time ago. It was in connection with a murder in the south of England, and during the immediate investigation my spirit guides were giving me a whole load of relevant information – names, part of a car number, even the clothes worn by the murderer. I passed it on and heard nothing; but some time later I was amazed to pick up a Sunday newspaper and read that a man had been arrested wearing exactly the outfit I had described.

I know there are some well documented cases in which mediums have been of help in solving crimes, but on the whole I don't really think the police take spiritual help very seriously. And from the medium's point of view, of course, it could be quite dangerous to get involved in, say, revealing figures in the underworld. It's not something that's anywhere near the top of my priority list.

I did once experience some really bad feelings and messages during a reading with one woman. I said: "The message I am getting is that you know someone who has committed a very bad crime, and you have covered up for him." She admitted that was indeed the case. It was one occasion where my bluntness came to the fore; I tore up the tape she was meant to take away with her, and told her in no uncertain terms that the reading had come to an end. That was far too heavy for me; I didn't want any of her friends knocking on my door.

In general I go along with that well-known medium Gordon Smith when he says the police generally wouldn't appreciate a medium taking the glory if they couldn't crack a case themselves. Mind you, I do think the police would benefit if they did take mediums a bit more seriously, for a practised medium can often just look at a group of people and tell who are the good guys and who are the baddies! I often get a feeling about people, and it has proved to be correct on so many occasions – which may not exactly be evidence as far as the law courts are concerned, but I am convinced there is some form of energy that the system is missing out on.

It is well known that America and Russia used to include "remote viewing", as telepathy is known, among the subjects for research during the Cold War period, and who knows what has gone on since those days. More recently the subject has been featured in the film "The Men Who Stare at Goats", starring George Clooney. Naturally the finished article has been embellished and drama- tised to make it a top attraction with cinemagoers, but there is no doubt the meat of the story is based on fact – that as far back as the 1970s the US Army formed a 1st Earth Battalion based in North Carolina made up of people with supposedly extraordinary psychic powers. Through the sheer strength of thought signals alone they attempted to knock over goats among other things in developing a technique that would be useful to the military, such as detecting enemy positions and even bringing down planes. Although there is no evidence that in their explorations they succeeded in these feats, there is no doubt there is substance in the story, confirmed by the likes of spoon-bender Uri Geller who has admitted links with US intelligence projects. And thanks to the Freedom of Information Act in the UK it is known that the British government has also been involved in remote viewing studies – not doing very well in soliciting the help of the best-known psychics, if reports are to be believed. But regardless of that, would governments waste time and money on employing top psychics if there was nothing in it? One day ... .

9 – Premonitional Dreams

I cannot remember exactly when I started to have premonitional dreams, but I did find the experience very disturbing. I would wake up with a bang and then re-live the episode, which stayed with me for ages. Sometimes it would be a matter of months before it meant anything, but then I would find the scene being enacted in real life. It must be part of The Gift; I cannot explain these things but I know there is a purpose behind them, so I just go with the flow.

Often the spirit messages come through when I am in a dream-like state. I used to keep a pad by my bedside and would write down any dreams immediately I woke up, even if it was in the middle of the night, because the likelihood is that they can be forgotten if you wait until the morning. Unfortunately I haven't kept those notes – if I had there would be a mountain of them by now! I'm the kind of person who can gather too much paper around me if I'm not careful, so I have to have de-cluttering spells now and again before I get overwhelmed by it all.

Some people have asked me to try and tell them the meaning of their dreams, but to be honest I have enough trouble interpreting my own. Look at all the books there are on the subject of dreams in high street book shops and libraries; if there was only one interpretation for each dream then there would be no market for all these writings. I do know that many dreams make no sense at the time, but may do at some point in the future after a certain happening; something will just click in the brain and you think: "Oh yes, now it all fits."

Personally, I don't remember my dreams very often. I think it has something to do with the state of the mind, and mine is usually still pretty active when I go to bed. I have trouble emptying my mind, maybe that is the problem!

I have never had a dream that involved anyone famous – except on one occasion that I will never forget. I received a warning in a dream about Princess Diana's accident before it happened, but I didn't quite know what I was seeing at the time. It was about two months before the tragedy in Paris, and it was a crazy dream – I couldn't make any sense of it, but the pictures were real enough in my mind when I woke up. I sat bolt upright and felt cold and clammy.

In the dream I was sitting in a cinema with Lady Di and she wanted me to accompany her outside. She kept saying: "I can't go on my own because they will keep following me." I said: "Don't be silly, I'll take you," and I could see myself walking with her. That dream made no sense to me until afterwards, and it didn't hit me until I was watching the funeral on television and saw the little white posy inscribed "To Mummy". Then I remembered the dream, and went weak at the knees. I said, "Oh my God." I realised it was her warning to me that she was afraid of being followed by the paparazzi. But what could I have done, anyway?

You see, dreams have to be deciphered. I've had many people describe their dreams to me, but it takes experience to work out the true meaning.

At the time I was first developing as a medium I was with Myvanwy, my Welsh mentor, when I saw the vision of a helicopter falling out of the sky and could clearly see these little bits of tin foil flying about. I said to Van, as we called her: "There's a man involved, and I can see the number 73." About a week later I was standing doing some ironing in front of the TV when the news came on and it showed the picture of a helicopter crashing out of the sky, with bits breaking off like confetti. They said a 73-year-old man had died in the accident.

I rang Van immediately, and she said: "I know what you are going to say. I've just seen it as well." I said: "I don't know if I'm cut out for this kind of work, I don't want to be picking up things like this all the time, all this doom and gloom. Is this what I'm going to be doing?" She said: "Don't worry, it won't be like this all the time. The spirit world is just letting you know that you have this vision." She talked me through it and calmed me down.

One of my most alarming premonitional experience came, not via a dream, but during an Automatic Writing session, when the following note appeared on my pad:

"September, September to remember,
 batten down the hatches, they will be despatched."

What was I suppose to make of that? It was quite a while before the Twin Towers catastrophe in America, which occurred on September 11, 2001, and will be forever etched into history as "9/11". I can only wonder why pieces of information like this do come through, because at the time it would not have meant anything to anybody. But was it some kind of message being sent through to me? I am as much in the dark as anyone else, I'm afraid, and can only contemplate in the aftermath.

10 – A Personal Quandary

A CUP AND SAUCER

A cup and saucer, a vessel for man to have a drink,
to refresh man, to make him think.
A cup of tea, a pint of beer,
make one which you prefer and have no fear.

Because God and the spirit world are watching over you,
watching everything you do in your every day to day.
God is watching so you are accountable,
you cannot run away.

Sometimes a request from people seeking readings can place the medium in a personal quandary. Should I relay the whole message as I have received it, even if the result might be quite painful? And should I even ask the question when there is the possibility of hurting someone?

The dilemma in which I found myself one day arose from a telephone call from Debbie, a lady I had seen before. She rang me up in tears wanting to make an appointment, and when she arrived she told me about her quandary – she had just heard from the doctor that she was five months pregnant, when she thought she was just going through the change of life! It was such a shock to her, but what made it even worse was the fact that doctors at the hospital were talking about the option of an abortion because of her age.

She wanted to know if I would make a link with her, and tell her what I could see. In fact I saw a baby on a scanner, and I could clearly see all its fingers and toes. I asked my guides about the baby's other organs, and was told they were perfect in every way. I told Debbie I could see a healthy little boy, but that the reading must be used for guidance purposes only, and that she had to make the final decision.

After she toddled off I promptly went to work on my guides. I shouted, ranted and raved, screaming at my main guide that I did not want to have the responsibility of helping someone choose between life and death. But I was merely told I would hear the outcome on the grapevine.

I got on with my work, pushing the incident to the back of my mind. It was about a year later before Debbie got in touch again, and over the phone I could hear baby noises in the background. "Babysitting tonight then, are we," I asked. "Don't you remember my reading, Maureen?" she asked, and then it all came flooding back to me.

My heart skipped a beat, but eventually I managed to ask: "Is the baby all right? Was he healthy?" She said: "He is perfect, sitting in his pram most of the time so well behaved that I don't know he's there." When she came to see me she showed me a picture on her mobile phone of a blond, blue-eyed boy looking like a little angel. "To think I nearly had him aborted," said Debbie.

That first reading put a real strain on me as a medium and a mother, but fortunately it turned out all right in the end. And the moral of the story came to light some 18 months later when I was sitting in a spiritualist church. The medium came over to me and said: "I am being told that you have been handing out a telling-off to your guides, giving them a hard time." I hung my head in shame and admitted she was right.

However, I learned a lot from that experience, not least because the trust in my guides went up 100 per cent. I sent up the thought that I was sorry – but I guess I passed the test! The spirits have on other occasions given me an insight into a pregnancy through the image of a pram, clearly visible to me when a woman has walked into my lounge for the first time. The vision indicates she is pregnant, or about to become pregnant, and more than once I have been able to pass on the news that a baby was on the way when they were completely unaware of their condition. I don't know if the news was good or bad, but I was proved right about the pregnancies.

When two young girls came to see me one evening I immediately linked with one of them. I could clearly see a baby around her and asked if she was pregnant, because I was picking up signs that indicated morning sickness. She became quite confrontational, and

I must admit it made me a bit wary. "I don't want a baby; I'm far too young," she shouted. But the signals to me were so strong that I just had to tell her what I was seeing (though I kept back the fact that the baby would be a little boy).

Later I learned in a phone call that she went straight out and bought a pregnancy test. Guess what – she was pregnant, and she later had a little boy called Kyle. I was told mother and baby were doing well.

Not everyone wants the kind of news that comes through me, but fortunately in that case it all turned out fine in the end.

I always tell it as it is, except when there is a death to be expected. I would never tell anyone about an imminent death, even if the details have come through to me – no self-respecting medium would do that. It is not our place to do that.

But I did have one lady, Rose, who said she had a premonition about her own passing, and asked me if I could pick it up. And I did – I saw a guide flicking up a light switch, which is their way of showing there is nothing to say, that life on this level is ending. But I didn't tell Rose the details. It is the only time I have ever seen a death in all the years I have been doing this work; maybe the spirits did this as a sort of test, to see how I would deal with it.

The situation left me so upset that I told another medium about it. She linked with my guides, and the message came back: "Well handled, caused no scandal."

The spirits are always testing me, and it really bugs me at times. But I think it is something that will always happen. I've just got used to it.

But apart from the life-and-death situations I never shirk to pass on the messages from the spirit guides, even if they are about personal relationships. When people come to me for a reading they give me permission to enter their energy fields and pick up what information I can; it's no good giving a medium that consent if you cannot take the truth!

I have been told that at times I can be a little blunt with that truth, but in my mind I am being painfully honest. "You tell it the way it is; you don't dress it up," some people have said, which I take as a compliment. Surely the truth is what we are all seeking.

I help people through healing and counselling skills that I have learned. But I never judge – I have certain gifts, but judging people is not one of them; that comes from a higher source.

I now realise my gift of mediumship was waiting for me, like a latent banana skin – an accident waiting to happen. I used to say to the spirit world: "Go away, leave me alone." I didn't ask for this to happen to me. But over the many years of my learning and testings I now accept this gift as an integral part of my life, and feel very privileged that I am one of the chosen few. I hope, most of all, that by taking time out to write a book it will give love and hope to people who, like me, have not led a very charmed life.

Occasionally I see more than one person at a single reading, though not as a general rule. One experience began with a visit by two sisters and, I don't know why, but something was telling me it was not a good thing to see them together, that I should split them up.

Fortunately they agreed to separate readings, and the first sister I saw was grateful that I did, for it turned out she had built up debts of some £23,000 and didn't want her sibling to know about them. However, I soon picked up on some large debts through the spirits, and she said to me afterwards: "I never dreamt you would talk about my huge debts. I'm so glad my sister was outside the room and not listening."

As I said, I'm not here to judge people, just to pass on the messages. In the case of these two sisters, both have been back to see me since then so they must have been impressed by what I was able to tell them.

Many of the people I see tend to treat me like a friend after a while; it is quite difficult to stay detached sometimes. I get to hear so many personal stories, and often I see different members of the same family. There was one occasion when the husband had died, and his family were all rowing and wrangling over who would pay for the headstone. One elder family member wanted to know what the younger one had said to me. I said: "Look, I'll read for you, but I can't get entangled in your family affairs." There are times when I have to be diplomatic but firm.

Another young lady called Diane came to see me in a very distraught state after having just lost her mother. She was an attractive woman, but I could see her loss was having a big effect on her. We completed a reading together, but it wasn't until she was about to leave that I received a vital piece of information from the mother. I was having a battle in my head – I didn't want to relay what I was seeing, and I kept saying to the mother, mentally: "I don't want to talk about that."

However, she persisted, so I told the daughter I had a message coming through about false teeth, of all things. I could see a tumbler with false teeth in it, and the mother was stirring them up with a metal spoon. I could distinctly hear the rattling noise it made, and in fact the mother kept telling me to use the word "rattle". I reluctantly passed on the message, with the result that the daughter broke down in tears.

When she had recovered she said: "I can't believe you just came out with that. I have been to several other mediums, but you are the first to pick up on those things." She explained: "When my mum was dying I said to her, 'If you can come back, please connect with me'. She pointed a finger and said, 'If I come back I'll rattle my false teeth at you'. You see, my mum's teeth never fitted so well after she became ill, and rattled when she spoke – it was a family joke."

That experience taught me that however stupid I think the message is, I must pass it on because it will obviously mean something to somebody. That young woman would have carried on searching, when in fact the evidence had come through. It proved to me once more that the spirit reigns supreme!

A really sad reading I gave was to a lady who had lost her young daughter when the car in which she was travelling hit a crash barrier. I was able to describe her dark hair, her features and the manner in which she conducted herself while she was on the Earth plain. When the mother gave me a locket to hold, I just knew it contained a lock of her daughter's hair, and I was right. The girl was such a good communicator that the mother was completely comforted in the knowledge she was at peace.

I was a little surprised that she never came back to see me, but I was overwhelmed by the number of people to whom she passed my name by way of recommendation. One of her friends told me: "That reading you gave her was such an in-depth one, it was everything she hoped for and gave her such a lot of comfort and healing." I felt so chuffed, because the mother and daughter were both so lovely. The woman was obviously able to move on with her life, and hopefully I have been able to bring reassurance to many of her friends and acquaintances ever since.

One lady came to me who had lost her young daughter with leukaemia, and she brought a little woolly hat the girl used to wear. Straightaway I saw the image of Snow White (without the seven dwarfs, I might add) standing on my lounge carpet in her yellow dress and blue cape, and asked what the connection was. The mother said: "My daughter bought this hat after seeing Snow White in Disneyland, and hardly ever took it off."

The spirit of the little girl was also showing me a teddy bear, and I noticed there was a little bear emblem on her hat. "She also bought a teddy bear on her holiday and we put that in her casket when she died," said the mother.

The lady admitted she wasn't handling the grieving process very well, which is understandable after losing a young daughter, but I'm pleased to say my readings and follow-up counselling did help her.

It is generally quite exhausting acting as a go-between for the spirits and the people they have left behind on Earth, and some readings can be quite personally painful to me. The visit of another young girl a few years ago was an example of the difficult dilemma in which I sometimes find myself.

After our reading I was seeing Kimberley to the door, saying our goodbyes, when my guide told me that the next time I saw her she would be in the spirit world, and that I would use her as my guide for her family.

It was obvious the girl was very ill at the time, and when her mother came to see me I was able to tell her that everything on the tape would mean something to her in six months time. The name Lorna kept coming through, but the mother said it meant nothing to her.

The girl eventually became gravely ill and went into a hospice, where the mother was introduced to her daughter's Macmillan nurse. "Hello, I'm Lorna," said the nurse. It was six months to the day since the original reading. "The hairs stood up on the back of my neck. I knew it was bad news," said the mother.

Some time after Kimberley's death her mother came to see me again – and it was an emotional time for both of us, because she was such a lovely girl. It was a very funny feeling for me especially, because I don't usually meet people on both sides of life.

It was another example of a very sad occasion, but when the daughter came through it did give comfort to the family. At the end of the day this is why I am so passionate about my work; it is the satisfaction I get from these experiences that drives me on.

11 – A Myriad of Reasons

Although I'm a medium first and foremost, many people seek my help as a clairvoyant. And in my book there is a difference. Mediumship is linking with the spirits to find comfort, while clairvoyance is the art of trying to put someone on their personal pathway. It's the same routine for me, but I must admit I like to know what people are expecting – contact with their loved ones or information about their pathway? I'm not asking for clues or seeking some kind of advantage, it's just that if they are heartbroken and need to make a connection, it's no good me going on for ages about how I see their future, and vice versa. People have different needs, and it's a fine line that I have to walk.

I don't mind dealing with sceptics, but people who are not very forthcoming and just sit back expecting me to do all the work are not helping their own cause. Any medium will tell you that a spirit is helped by hearing the sound of a voice; a person who has a negative attitude and just offers a few mumbled responses is in effect blocking the spirit – and, by the same token, blocking my attempts to help them link up. It is naturally easier to work with a person who is being more open.

Sometimes I am on the other end of people's problems – those in marriage triangles seem to crop up all the time, and I am told that Internet chat rooms are the root cause of quite a few of today's troubles. One woman who came to see me had broken up her marriage before she had even met the person she had been chatting to – can you believe that! Talk about chasing foolish dreams.

Then there are young men (and women) who don't seem too sure of their own gender. Sometimes I sit down after a reading and think: My God, what a web we weave when wishing to deceive. Now and again I think perhaps I am missing out on some of life's excitement, but in my heart I know I have to keep my feet firmly planted on the ground in order to stay in control and continue my work. The stance I once took – "Hang on a minute, I don't want all this responsibility" – went out of the window a long time ago. I have learned to carry on regardless, hoping in some small way to help change the scheme of things; and I really feel flattered that people take me into their confidence.

People are hurting for a myriad of reasons, and it is not always self-inflicted. But I do believe we have to be shown lessons about living, loving and life – it is all about the soul's progression. As I am able to give proof of the spirit world to many people in my own small way, hopefully little seeds are planted that will germinate and grow, enabling many more to become aware of other life forces on our precious planet.

It has taken a lot of learning and soul searching on my part, but I have learned how to blend with the energies of the spirits. However, I still have to point out to clients that our readings together are often only guidance and should not be used as a platform on which to base their whole life. Our loved ones who have passed are not allowed to live our lives for us on this Earth plane – that is why they show us only snippets. I cannot emphasise enough that it is us who must take the overall responsibility.

I must admit though that I don't get the same satisfaction from clairvoyant readings as I do from mediumship. When a lady left my house the other day, obviously so relieved and comforted by the news I was able to give her, I just felt like raising my arms and shouting like a footballer who has just scored an important goal. It is so rewarding to be able to bring happiness to people.

As I have said, the most common reason for people to seek a medium is obviously to find some solace after losing a loved one, but it's not just one type of person – I've met people from all walks of like, across the whole spectrum, and their reasons for coming can be as varied as the weather.

Some have very preconceived ideas, turning up holding a loved one's wedding ring, for example, and say they want to speak to their wife/husband/mother. I have to explain very tactfully that I am merely an instrument for messages, like a telephone receiver, and that it is not like going to Sainsbury's with a shopping list. It doesn't work like that – I can't choose who will come through, it is all engineered by the spirit world. Now and again several spirits will try and come through at once, which isn't the easiest situation to control when there is a simultaneous conversation going on with the client. I simply send up the message: "Come on, sort yourselves out," and it usually works!

Some people are more interested in the philosophy behind spiritualism, and I don't mind this kind of meeting because I can talk for England on the subject. Sometimes people want their own "gift" confirmed by an outsider; one young woman has been to me several times, and I know she has psychic powers, but she is petrified about what she sees and needs to be coaxed into recognising and using these powers. Some new beginners don't have the willpower or the experience to maintain a balanced lifestyle, which I think is important, otherwise they can get carried away with their new-found abilities and it will have a draining effect on their own spirit.

Maybe I shouldn't say this about my work, but there is a tedious side to it sometimes. Would you believe that teenage girls come to me and ask if they are going to be famous, or how they should go about achieving some sort of fame. Perhaps it's something to do with the quality of the reality TV programmes of today, but it's such a sad reflection on our times that these youngsters will go to almost any depths to reach a celebrity status rather than work at a skill or carve out a career!

Mind you, there have been occasions when visits to me have foretold of rewarding relationships and work moves. When one woman came to me with her daughter, a young model, I relayed the letter "J" that kept appearing in my mind. She left muttering that she didn't believe a word she had heard, but three months later she did meet a famous showbusiness star whose name began with a J – I won't embarrass him by naming him – and it led to a fantastic modelling contract.

Often these things don't happen overnight; it can take months and even years, but I have had so many return visits from people saying that my messages to them have turned out to be true. They cannot all be coincidences!

I guess mediums are always being asked to confirm certain facts and sort out relationships, but unfortunately it doesn't always work on that level. When I get an initial, people want a name, and sometimes I get Christian names and surnames and am able to piece the facts together – but it doesn't always come through in the way they hope. I can't say to the spirits: "Give me a name, give me an address." I'm only an open channel for their communications. Would you believe that I've had people trying to test me by asking me what colour underwear they have on. What's that all about!

In my early learning days all I ever seemed to get through were names, and to be perfectly honest I found it rather boring. I said to Myvanwy, my main teacher: "I'm getting a bit fed up with this, I don't think I want to carry on with this work." She said: "It won't always be like this, you will be able to pick up on other things if you persevere."

And so it proved. But why doesn't a spirit come through with more specific information, such as a full address with postcode? That would be very helpful. I can't really explain why, all I can say is that sometimes names do come through loud and clear. It is dependent on the energies developed at the time, but I must say that when the information from the spirits proves to be correct – and I get a lot of feedback from clients who say it invariably is – then it is very rewarding.

The spirits have often helped me find material things for people. One woman said to me after a reading: "I don't suppose you can find my ring for me. I've searched the house and can't find it anywhere." The vision I kept getting was of a hand feeling down the back of a chest of drawers, but when I told her she said she didn't have any furniture like that in her home. It must have been some two years later when she came back and pressed a ring into my hand – I often ask for a personal possession at readings to aid the psychometry. I said: "What a beautiful ring," and she replied: "Yes, and it's thanks to you that I have it." To be honest, I didn't remember the original meeting until she jogged my memory; it's difficult to remember details about everyone when I'm seeing so many different people each week. "You told me about a chest of drawers," she said, "and some time later I realised there was one at my dad's house. Next time I went there I felt down the back – and there was the ring."

For one woman the real meat of the message was much closer to home than she ever expected. She wanted to know if there was a man about to enter her life, and the signal I kept getting was: "He's over there. He's over there." It didn't mean much to her at the time, but a while later she came running up to me when I was doing some shopping in the local supermarket. "You were dead right. The man turned out to live in the next street," she said, showing me a large engagement ring. And the man was in fact a former childhood sweetheart; they had lost touch and she didn't know he was living so close

Some youngsters also want my help in finding out about how certain relationships will work out. They have maybe been in a bad relationship, but want me to tell them that the situation will change; well the bad news is that it probably won't. One woman had been the mistress in a triangular relationship for no less than 13 years, and asked me when she would finally live with the husband. I had to give her the message that it wouldn't happen, but she should not have needed a medium for that kind of information. That part of my work can be quite tiresome.

Some people may be surprised to learn that quite a few business people come for a reading, wanting to know if their ideas are going to be a success. Some are already millionaires, but they still want a take "from above" on the next big deal before they put pen to paper. Others are sceptics, but still can't resist trying to look into the future.

I think the 2008-9 recession has been a boon to mediums – something that national surveys unsurprisingly failed to recognise when talking about which parts of the economy somehow benefited from the worldwide slow-down. You would be surprised how many business people consult a medium before making a major decision, and naturally people are even more scared than usual of making financial mistakes when the climate is so bad. I have had men who want to know whether it would be a good time for the expansion they have in mind, or whether bankruptcy signs lie ahead. Usually they just want reassurance that they are on the right track; it's what I call a Corporate reading, which is entirely different to dealing with a bereavement.

When I gave a reading to Judy, a woman from London, much of the talk was about her husband's business interests. She took home a tape of the meeting, as most of my clients do, and her husband just could not believe some of the facts that were coming out. "How on earth could she know that?" he exclaimed, and promptly booked a session with me himself. I was able to set his mind at rest about his multi-million-pound expansion plans – as I helped another very wealthy client who exports goods to Japan. He was seeking help about a complex court case in which he was involved, and the information he received through me turned out to be true.

Usually he would turn up for a reading dressed very informally, in fact I would describe his outfits as flamboyant, sometimes even with Hawaiin-style shirts. But on one particular occasion he was all in black – shoes, shirt, tie, jacket, the lot. I couldn't help notice the difference from his usual dress sense, and to be honest it was making me feel a little uncomfortable. I had to mention it to him – "Why are you dressed in black today?" I asked. "I don't know, Maureen," he said, "I just felt the urge to put these on today."

It looked like a mourning outfit to me, and when he said he was planning his next overseas trip to Thailand, I said: "I don't want you to go. It's just a feeling I have." A few weeks later that awful tsunami struck in the Indian Ocean in December 2004, and from the news reports I knew that if he had been in the particular region of Thailand where he was planning to go, he would be lucky to escape with his life. I was overcome with worry, and tried to telephone him and his family to find out if he was all right, but without success. Then a while later he phoned me: "It's OK, Maureen," he said, "I didn't go. It didn't feel right after what you told me. But I must tell you this – the hotel I would have stayed in was hit by the tsunami and destroyed!"

Neither of us can explain why he dressed in black that day, why it made me feel uneasy, or why he heeded my warning and changed his travel plans. It was a weird reading, and although it had a happy ending as far as my client's life was concerned, there was a traumatic twist when he discovered his girlfriend in Thailand was on the missing list. "I think you have to assume she perished that day," I said.

I've also had women asking about how many children they will have, and the predictions have proved right. Among the many

Christmas cards I get every year is one from a lady at Weston-super-Mare who asked me if she was making the right house move; I was able to tell her "Yes", and she has been thanking me ever since she moved into the bungalow that I described to her many years ago.

As I started to meet more people through my readings, it made me realise how difficult life is for many of us. I have seen many ladies who have been diagnosed with cancer and are waiting for the all-clear; many are obviously fearful and desperate for someone to talk to. Other clients have been receiving fertility treatment – which not only puts a strain on the physical relationship because of the waiting and uncertainty involved, but also in many cases the cost of treatment imposes financial hardship. We all want something we can't have, but those cases are heart-rending. I tell them: "There is a lot of hurt in this world, but try to make sure you are not a part of it. Think of the love you have and the good things in your life."

It is also sad when people come to me following a suicide in the family, especially when the person ended their life at quite a young age. But the ones my heart goes out to the most are those who have lost a little child; the sheer tenacity in trying to cope with their loss and grief is such a heavy burden to bear. I tend to dread these readings in a way but, as the evidence comes through, the love that is felt is quite inspiring. I can't help but learn from them, and the fact that I have played my part in some way, helping the parents to cope with their bereavement, is quite uplifting.

It is never easy relaying messages from a child, and I often end up with a big lump in my throat. But I never shy away from them because more often than not these little spirits are very loving and forgiving, and they often result in very lively readings. I remember one husband and wife who came to me after they lost their four-year-old daughter in a pond drowning accident. The man was a sceptic through and through – and I never mind meeting sceptics, because at least they have an open mind – but as the evidence poured through from the child's spirit he was in tears.

Afterwards he apologised for his doubting attitude and said he was ashamed of himself. "Why do you do this work, it must be so upsetting for you," he said, but I told him that although it was indeed very sad to read for a child, the love and gratitude of his daughter – and from the spirit friends and the parents – made it all worthwhile for me. He came in with a heavy heart, but left in good spirits, talking about his little girl as if she was still close to him. To be able to channel this love is the highest reward for me.

A fellow medium told me years ago I would one day carry out bereavement counselling, but I said I didn't think so because I would find it so depressing. I know now that was the voice of ignorance, because it is in fact one of the most rewarding tasks I have ever accomplished. Now I know I am hooked and could never move away from my work, which has become a way of life. Once again the spirits have reigned supreme, for they must have an insight into what we mere mortals are capable of, and use us as instruments for the betterment of man.

It's a fact that most people seek out a medium to find some sort of comfort after losing a loved one, but there are those who want to find out more about themselves and look into the future. This is where the clairvoyance aspect kicks in, and there's no harm in that because we are all seeking and searching for answers; we all want to better ourselves and to have a better life, there's nothing wrong with that attitude. But if someone wants to live their life through a medium, I am afraid most people in my line of work will recognise what is happening and pull the plug on the situation.

People have said to me: "Can you give me a definite answer; can you tell me what I must do?" The answer is "No." I would be taking their own free will away from them, and that is not what the spirit world does. Everyone has their own free will and their choices in life – the spirit will only guide. I believe we are all put on this Earth plane to learn and to evolve our own spirit, and no-one else can do that for us.

Unfortunately a medium cannot always choose the kind of people who want to meet them; it is just one facet of the job, and the energy take-up is the reason why I cannot see too many people in a single day or even a week. It is part of my philosophy for life that I would rather do one or two readings that are successful and rewarding to the client, than do three or more that are a bit iffy. If my work ever became shoddy, I wouldn't want to do it any more. It's different for Tarot readers, they just sit there and interpret the cards – but that is not what I do.

One reason why some people turn to a medium is to unburden their own guilt; maybe they feel they have treated someone badly, or perhaps there has been an incident that began as an argument and developed into a long-standing grudge. These things happen in life, but when one person passes over often the remaining party is left with the guilt. Now and again someone will turn up wanting to put a family feud to rest, yearning for closure and even begging forgiveness. At first they may be wary of admitting their part in the falling-out, but I have picked up on quarrels and told them: "The person who has passed over is worrying about this matter as much as you are. You both need to forgive."

I have also had clients who need closure with people still living regarding disputes that have caused bad blood. One lady came back and told me that after my advice she did heal a rift with her mother – who died a few months later. "I'm so glad we made it up before it was too late," she said, and agreed that failure to do so would have left her with a nasty taste in the mouth for the rest of her life.

Unexpected deaths are another cause of guilt. "I never had the chance to say the things I wanted to say, or even to say goodbye properly," is a common theme, and quickly reduces people to tears. "I never visited as much as I should have done, and never saw him/her in the days shortly before the death," is another guilt feeling expressed to me on a regular basis. I just tell them: "That's baggage that carries quite a negative energy. You have to learn to put that to one side, because when people enter the spirit world they don't take their baggage with them." Spirits have a love vibration; I've never had one yet that comes to me and says: She didn't visit me enough, or didn't do this or that.

One of the most common reasons for guilt when someone has died these days is the care home factor. With people generally living longer, but not in the small family enclaves of yesteryear, many feel guilty about their parents spending the last few remaining years of their lives in a care home. For whatever reason – maybe a lack of space, distance or any number of personal reasons – the sons and daughters often just cannot cope with the situation and a place in a care/rest/nursing home is deemed the best solution, if not the perfect one. They know the staff will generally do their best, and maybe in many cases the elderly are quite happy to live out their final years surrounded by people of a like age and with similar circumstances. However, the kind of scenario where an elderly relative has dementia or Alzheimer's Disease seems to occur in my readings on a regular basis, and even decisions made with the best of intentions can still leave a feeling of guilt when death finally occurs.

I have had people who are absolutely heartbroken and crying their eyes out. "I had to put my father in an old people's home, do you think I did the right thing, has he forgiven me?" is a message I have had to send on many times. Just recently the vision I received back from a deceased father was one of oxygen tanks and masks. I said: "He needed medical attention and you could not have given him that at home. He is telling me he fully understands why you made the decisions you did." But some children – who themselves are often middle-aged and sometimes even getting into old age themselves – need quite a lot of counselling and convincing before the guilt passes.

On a much lighter note, I do get the odd person who wants to know something like next Saturday's winning Lottery numbers – I would be a rich woman if I had a pound for every time that subject has been mentioned. I just have to explain that the spirit world is only interested in our spiritual wellbeing, health and happiness, and pays no attention to our material requests. Those are the occasions when I have to be blunt and put them in their place.

I know one famous medium who tells the story about a huge win in a casino, but I tend to doubt stories like that. If mediums could forecast things like that we would all be queueing up to have a dip at the jackpot, or taking the Lottery prizes home.

Mind you, I have seen money around some clients, and in fact I actually did see some bingo numbers around one lady called Kath, and she laughed and said: "Well, I am always going down to the Bingo hall." I said: "You are going to win in the run-up to

Christmas, but it won't be a big win, something in the region of £200." Next time I saw her, guess what she said: "Hey Maureen, I won £250 at the Bingo, and we had a nice Christmas out of it."

Another reading that involved money and had a happy ending was with an older widow named Ann. However, the session didn't start so well for her when the spirit of her husband came through and was giving her some real stick; in fact I had to tone down some of his remarks for fear of upsetting her too much, especially having regard to her frail state of mind at the time. She was rebuked for trying to cope on her own and not accepting help in the home, which she obviously needed because of her age and her poor health. But there was a heartening communication about the thing that was almost driving her out of her mind with worry – a £400 tax bill. She was told not to lose any sleep over the demand and that the situation would sort itself out. I must admit my first thought was the same as Ann's – it's easy for someone to say such a thing, but it's hard to put it out of your mind when you are getting on in years, have a limited income and are suddenly faced with a large bill.

I know I have faith in the spirits, but even I could hardly believe my ears when she rang me the very next day. "You'll never believe what I have just received in the post," said Ann. "It's a letter telling me the £400 demand was a mistake." One hugely relieved and happy client!

Charlotte was another woman who came to me with an admittance of spending too much money. Apparently she was obsessed by the work of mediums, had been to see every one in her home region and had rung up massive phone bills by contacting all the advertised psychic lines. She had to admit that the messages and advice I gave her were similar to what she had been told before – but that was not what she wanted to hear.

"You are right regarding the details of my current relationship," she said. So I replied: "When are you going to listen, then?" She said she was with a man who was very abusive, but she needed to hear that he would change his ways and that she would live with him happily ever after. "I am afraid that is not going to happen. It is not the truth of the situation as I am being shown," I said.

I didn't like to tell her that the man was rotten to the core; she must have realised that herself, but wanted someone to sympathise with her and tell her it would all come good in the end. In situations like that I have to stand back as a human being and not act as judge, jury and executioner, but merely counsel and advise.

Fortunately those kind of clients are quite rare, and the vast majority of people who seek guidance from me are good citizens who take the spiritual messages on board in the way they are meant to be absorbed.

12 – Children and Angels

A CHRISTENING

A baby is being Christened today,
all the posh hats come out to play.
This little baby marks new life,
a respite for its mother from toil and strife.

She is one of God's gifts, so as you gather round the font,
take a look at all the glee, feel the love and humanity.
This truly is a wonderful day
as all the angels come out to play.

One of the ideas still floating around in my head is a book of children's stories, and one medium I saw soon picked up on this many years ago. She said: "You have carried out a reading for a child in the spirit world, haven't you," and I had to admit I had. She said: "That book inside of you is aimed at the under eight-year-olds, and I think you know where it is coming from."

Indeed I do. I feel it is coming from the young boy I referred to at the beginning of my story, the one who died after visiting Disneyland. His mother has been back to see me, and I feel very strongly that he is still around me.

When she first came to see me I had immediately connected with the spirit of this small boy. I glimpsed him out of the corner of my eye – a dear little soul and a lively character, talking so fast that it was a job to keep up with him. "That is my mummy and you are going to tell her how much I love her," he said. A tear fell from the cheek of the mother when I relayed the message. This is how the conversation then proceeded.

> MEDIUM: "He is making me aware of his little head, telling me that he has no hair and has a bad head."

> MOTHER: "That is correct. He went over with a brain tumour."

83

MEDIUM: "He is writing the number seven in the air. Does this have any significance?"

MOTHER: "He was aged seven when he passed."

MEDIUM: "He is now making me laugh; he is trying to ride a scooter but I am afraid he is not having much luck and has just dropped the machine and walked off. I think he has given it up as a bad job."

MOTHER: "He never did learn to ride his scooter. It was his last Christmas present, but it was a bit big for him." (Her tears turned to tears of joy as she talked about her memories with the child.)

MEDIUM: "I now have a lady here who is fiercely knitting as if her whole life depended on this article getting finished. I can clearly see the knitting needles and can hear them clicking."

MOTHER: "You are correct, but can you give me more evidence?"

MEDIUM: "Why am I seeing, of all things, an Aunt Sally doll with rosy cheeks that belong to Worzel Gummage?" (More tears)

MOTHER "Do you want me to tell you, because you are correct!"

MEDIUM: "No, I will tell you what I am picking up. Your little boy tells me this was put into his casket, and that his grandmother had stayed up all night to finish it in time so he could have it with him."

MOTHER: "This is all correct. I cannot thank you enough. My sister and I made a pact that neither of us would put any pressure on you, and I was taken aback when my son was the first thing you talked about. This is our ultimate proof."

That wasn't quite the end of the story, because my daughter later told me she had a film of the Disney "Small World" complex. I know I was being shown this tape for a reason, and naturally there were more tears. But there was still another personal chapter to add to this story, because one year later I visited Disneyland with my daughter and grandchildren, and experienced the Small World rides for myself. There was a sad element to it, however, because there were many children around who were obviously ill, quite a few in wheelchairs. But I could see why they wanted to go there and, my God, weren't they enjoying themselves. It was magical.

The mother had told me that the little boy drove her mad by incessantly singing "It's a small world". Now I understood why, and sent up a little healing prayer.

One of my poems, entitled "A Christening", is for all the new children who will come to our planet. I do think children are generally more psychic than adults. I still remember a couple of incidents that happened when I was aged about nine years old, one involving an old-fashioned wooden chest of drawers. I saw one of the long drawers open up and a person sat up in it; I described to my Mum the face I saw, a man with a large Jimmy Edwards-style bushy moustache, and she said matter-of-factly that it was my grandfather. Later on she showed me some old family photographs – which I swear I had never seen before – and there was her father's face just as I had described it.

But however psychic children might be, I won't allow them in during a reading. People have sometimes asked me if their youngsters could sit in with them, but I have to tell them I would find it far too distracting. And although some mediums do hold readings for children, I will not take a booking unless the person has reached the upper-teens age.

Now and again I have been asked if I think a client's son or daughter will be successful in following a certain career, and of course I do my best to get answers to their questions. And before the cynics rise up, let me emphasise it's nothing to do with fortune-telling, it is simply finding a spiritual guide to a pathway reading for a child who is not present. I remember telling one parent I could see her small son kicking a ball – which in itself, granted, is not an unusual pursuit for a boy. But I could see that he was exceptionally gifted at the sport and would go on to make money as a professional player, which is unusual, and I was proved right.

I also believe the spirits are often at work when children claim they see fairies (or elemental spirits, as they are known) at the bottom of the garden, or they are able to perform extraordinary feats. Take a six-year-old child prodigy who can paint like a master or play the piano like Beethoven when they are hardly big enough to clamber onto the piano stool. Is this really possible without some spiritual guidance? I don't think so.

I was giving a reading to a woman one day and I said: "I believe you have a very gifted child. Why can I see a small boy, aged about five or six, and a bar billiards table? He doesn't look big enough to see over the top of the table without standing on a chair. That's crazy." She said: "No, it's not crazy. My son is just six, and he can beat all the men in the local bar."

Children are very perceptive and have that sixth sense. I know my daughter and I had great fun watching my little grandchild playing with her tea service and talking to little people that only she could see. Or could she? We just don't know, do we? I believe it is more than just their imagination working overtime, but they cannot understand why everyone doesn't see things from their point of view. When they get to the age of nine or ten children usually get this sixth sense knocked out of them by adults saying: "Don't be so stupid, of course you didn't see anything."

I often get asked if I believe in angels, and I am not embarrassed to admit I do. They may not come in the form of James Stewart's angel in the famous film *It's A Wonderful Life*, still a Christmas favourite after more than 60 years, but I firmly believe someone is watching over us in one way or another and helping to guide us. How many times have you been in a situation where you think you should turn right, but then at the last moment something tells you to turn left, and that proves correct. This inner knowledge that we find so hard to explain has often saved a life or kept a person out of danger. You can call it what you like, but I believe there are higher beings of light – a divine intervention if you like – that help to keep us safe.

"Do Angels exist" was one of the recent topics on the BBC's Sunday morning programme *The Big Questions*, when it was revealed the majority of people do believe in some form of guardian angel – even those who have no religious faith – and leading members of the Christian and Muslim faiths had to admit there are many references to angels in both the Bible and the Koran. With Prof David Jones – who has taken on the task of writing a history of angels for his latest book – joining in the debate, the general consensus seemed to be that believing in such things can only lead to a better view on life; and I can't argue with that.

Some mediums even specialise in the subject of angels and hold workshops for both believers and sceptics. The message is usually the same: that there are millions of guardian angels around who are serving the divine power – again call it God or whatever you want – by helping to keep us safe, conquer fear and deliver hope. Although I don't go in for these group sessions myself, I am certainly not against the idea and feel that any genuine processes that help to break down barriers and open up the public's awareness of the psychic world can only be a good thing.

I once asked my spirit guides to show me something angelic and, as often happens, there was no immediate response. But a little while later I was sitting in the garden reading a newspaper when a tiny feather floated down and settled on the centre pages. Was this a coincidence?

Mediums say the angels appear in many different forms, sometimes in a pleasant human shape, sometimes even with wings. They mostly appear to me as hazy beams of light, but one reading I did for a lady called Doreen proved particularly memorable, for it was the only time I have seen a being of pure light, and in the traditional angelic form complete with wings. The figure seemed about 12 feet tall and lit up the whole room, but it brought with it an encompassing feeling of overwhelming love – we both felt the effect of this vision. Doreen then explained that her mother had recently passed away, and her children had since referred to her as "Nanny angel in the sky", buying a new angel for the Christmas tree to commemorate her. Whatever I witnessed and felt that day, I know it wasn't Earthly. Try telling me it wasn't the love of an angel!

13 – Success as a Healer

AN ANGEL

An angel flew around on God's land,
very tiny and pixie like,
Throwing out her magic dust,
trying to free man from greed and lust.

We do not know she is there
because we cannot see her.
But mark my word, my friend,
she is there.

Doing God's work, healing the sick,
praying for the hurt.
She is a spirit sent by God
to help the world do its job.

There must be as many different types of healing being practised as there are countries on this Earth. Besides the popular
methods such as Reiki and Hypnotherapy, there is Homeopathy,
Reflexology, Vortex Healing, Crystal Healing, Acupuncture,
Indian Head Massage, Aromatherapy, IET (Integrated Energy
Theory), Craniosacral therapy that takes a holistic approach
incorporating "an appreciation of body, mind and spirit" ... I
could go on and on.

I have attended sessions on some of these alternative health
methods simply because many of them are connected to spiritualism, and I find the whole range fascinating; some arts are based
on the scientific and medical knowledge of bone and muscle struc-
ture, but many simply get their energy from a God-force of some
kind. There have been times when I have been disappointed at both
the execution of the healing method and the result, but sometimes
I have emerged feeling much brighter - which means a success in
my book.

Soon after I moved house I received a reiki healing session for the first time, and I must admit I was amazed at the result. The energy I felt was so strong, my whole body seemed to be vibrating. I was lying on a couch but I felt as if I was in orbit. It was a very spiritual journey, and I certainly slept well that night. Even the next day I was feeling the benefit – it felt as if a sheet of cling film had been taken off my head. As with every profession in life, there are good and bad examples, and I must have chosen a good one for that session. The experience left me so relaxed and at one with myself, I could not praise the healer enough. She was definitely able to call on a higher energy; I just know something else was at work that night.

I believe many of the so-called "miracle" cures make their way onto this plane from the spirits of doctors, nurses, scientists – all sorts of learned people who have departed and who retain the knowledge and experience to help us mere mortals.

One woman came to me shortly before having to undergo a hospital operation, and she was really scared. Let's face it, most of us are when confronted with a major health scare and the operating table. During her reading I could actually see her spiritual guides, and I told her before she left that they were actively around her. Later I was told by the husband that she had a very sound sleep the night before going into hospital – and that was really unusual! "She was amazingly calm, I can't thank you enough," he said. I just reiterated that the spirit guides had been at work; they sent her to me and they were then able to transmit a calming, healing process. There have been many occasions when I have been able to help on the healing side without even touching the person; the guides know when they are needed.

Another lady called Stella came to me for a healing session after acid reflux turned into a large tumour and she couldn't digest her food. Again I could see the guides at work – as soon as I put my hands on her head I could feel something being wrung out. Her arms began visibly shaking and I could sense all kind of things were going on in her body; she said she could feel her muscles shaking. When she went back for an X-ray she was told by the nurse: "This doesn't make a lot of sense. A large tumour showed up on your last visit, but in the last two weeks it has shrunk so much that we can hardly detect it."

She told me later that she was in two minds as to whether to tell the nursing staff about her visit to a medium, because she didn't know how they would react. After a lot of thought she did tell them and they agreed that something remarkable had taken place. Later I learned from her sister that she had undergone a further bout of chemotherapy and had been given the all-clear, and the last news I heard was that she was managing to eat solid food again.

It's a fact that many hypnotherapists believe that the majority of illnesses are psychosomatic, meaning they arise out of the unconscious mind, physical illnesses created by our mental state rather than by germs and viruses. If this is true, it provides an awful lot of work for the 'mind doctors', and with the stress that life today puts on the human body, I can only see the list of practices getting even longer.

Obviously healing does work on many levels; my own work is all the proof I need of that. But it will probably be a long time before faith healers are generally taken seriously by the orthodox medical profession. Waiting for praise from that quarter is a bit of a thankless task – that's my experience.

While out shopping in my local supermarket I bumped into a lady who had been for readings on several occasions. What was special was the fact that Anna had a baby boy in a pushchair – the baby that I had predicted she would have! That gave me a funny feeling, meeting the child that I had a premonition about several years before, but it's always a bonus when I actually get to meet a child under those circumstances.

She also thanked me for helping one of her cousins. The man had been mixing with someone who proved to be a very bad influence, dabbling with drugs and so on, and apparently I had even named his supplier. I couldn't remember the details of the reading, but by all accounts I had given him a bit of an ear-bashing, for which I apologised. "Oh no," said Anna, "he definitely needed a kick up the backside, and you gave it to him. You even named the person who was causing the trouble, and that freaked him out. But he did listen, and having dropped the person like a stone he is much happier and managing to steer clear of trouble."

This again is the power of the spirit world working in a mysterious way, but the result was a good one with another soul sorted out. To me, it's another example of healing – as was the session I experienced with Bella, one of the few clients I have received who is totally deaf.

My powers of communication were put to the test in that reading, but by exaggerated lip and arm movements I was able to convey the messages to Bella that, although she was full of grief after recently losing a baby, I was certain she would later have a healthy baby girl. I'm still waiting to hear the latest news from her, so it's a case of "watch this space", but I am fully confident the guides will be proved right once again.

To give a better insight into my own form of healing, before a client arrives I go into a trance – but only a light "overshadowed" state, and the client also usually drifts off into a kind of light sleep. Is it hypnotism? I don't really think so, I certainly haven't learnt or practised hypnotism. It's the same with the mediumship and psychology arts, it is all instinct on my part. I do put on a meditation tape, usually with some beautiful tranquil music, and I say: "Just listen to the music, forget all your cares and go to sleep if you want to." I can then tell if they have drifted off, and if so I gently bring them back.

I don't go into a deep trance, because obviously I wouldn't be able to carry on without a third person if I did. Some mediums do have a secretary or helper to make notes for them while in a trance, but I prefer to work on my own; just stand back and let it all happen. Basically the spirits are using me as a conduit – all they want from me is my voice box.

I know many reiki exponents who don't actually touch their clients at all, they just put their hands to within a few inches of the client and can still feel the energy pass through. But my method is to place my hands on the person's head, the crown, and he or she will then feel an energy coming up from the soles of their feet. The feeling I have is of following instructions. We all have meridian lines in our bodies, the Chinese realised this centuries ago.

I have had a lot of success with this type of healing. I remember in the early days a medium said to me: "Maureen, you can heal people without getting out of your chair." I didn't know what he meant, but it is a fact that I am able to go into a light trance through meditation – and all I know is that it works!

When I first came to the Swindon area I worked with a colleague called Ken who was suffering from cancer, and I carried out a healing session with him. "Can I ask you a question?" he said afterwards. I said, "I think I know what you are going to ask." He said: "How can you heal my feet and my head at the same time?" I said: "I have been asked that many times. I put my hands on your head, and you can sense my touch there, but the vibes come up through the feet. That's the proof that it's not me doing the healing." All I do is invite the spirit guides, then I believe the doctors and healers who were formerly in this world are continuing to do their work.

Of course there are sharks and con merchants lurking about in every profession, so the client has to remain street-wise. In my younger days I had a nasty experience with a male so-called healer, and I have heard stories from other women who have felt uncomfortable with mediums who practise hypnotism and healing. Some forms of healing do not necessitate any touching whatsoever, while other practices may vary. I just know how I feel – I wouldn't want to be put in a position where I was not in control of my own mind and movements, so my advice to anyone who feels at all uneasy in a session is to get yourself out of that situation as quickly as possible.

During my learning years I sometimes experienced working in harmony with other mediums in healing groups, and I can verify the fact that putting several heads together can create a very powerful force.

One of the best examples of healing through collective thought and prayer is the Tibetan monk. These country people spend much of their life in quiet contemplation, all dressed in the same orange coloured clothes, which results in all members being at one with each other – there's no petty jealousies, rivalry or keeping up with the Joneses. They do go about their work from a different vantage point to us, and when I was younger I must admit I used to think their lifestyle was a bit of a waste; it is only since I have got a bit older and wiser that I have begun to see the logic of their well-ordered life.

The whole population of Tibet is only some one or two million, depending on the source of information, and although Buddhism is not the only religion practised in the land, one third of the people do become monks. Only since the Fifties has it been under the rule of the Chinese, who have attempted to destroy or change the culture and consciousness of this mountainous people – but without success! Through their lifestyle of high moral values the monks are considered to be the ultimate followers of Buddha, showing a level of contentment rarely seen in other parts of the world. Maybe the fact that their way of life does not include many of the stresses of the modern Western world also helps them to live longer than the average, but it is their philosophy of mind over matter that really intrigues me – they are able to control their minds to the extent of shutting out pain while walking on burning coals and carrying out other feats of superhuman strength. We have evidence of the mind's working from people who have had limbs amputated; they will tell you they still sometimes feel real pain from those limbs because the brain still believes the limbs are in place. That is a demonstration of the power of the mind.

14 – My Red Indian Guide

Many mediums seem to have an Aztec Indian or someone of Native American descent as one of their spirit guides. I suppose it has something to do with the fact that the tribes of that era were much more in touch with the powers of extra sensory perception than we seem to be today. Historians have often wondered how tribes could communicate across oceans, and ESP appears to be the most logical answer. Also, the Red Indians were very in touch with nature – they couldn't go into a chemist's shop when someone was ill, they used natural products that came out of the ground for medicine. And by putting their ears to the ground they could tell a lot about who was in the vicinity. They were very in tune with Mother Earth, and had men who were full of learning and philosophy – that is why it is no coincidence that they continue to communicate from the spirit world.

So you will not be surprised to learn that I have my own Red Indian guide – he is called Proudfoot and was a member of the Pawnee tribe, which is described by some historians as "the most amazing American Indian tribe ever". They are known to have lived in mud huts (not tepees) in New Mexico during the 16th century and migrated north to Nebraska, where they traded with the early European settlers rather than fight with them. Although their buffalo hunting grounds were gradually diminished by the incursion of the white man, many Pawnee braves acted as scouts for the US Army in the 19th century. But they did have some peculiar traits – for instance, they were one of the few tribes to practice the human sacrifice of young girls to appease certain gods, and also believed certain animals had magical powers, including the ferret for some reason! The women were the field workers, tending the crops as in China, while the males took on the role of hunter-gatherers, decision makers and medicine men.

I know Proudfoot is a medicine man. He only comes through to me when I am meditating or in a trance state, although I don't receive any specific messages or information from him. He just lets me know he is around me and is offering his support; he calms me down and gives me balance. Then during hands-on healing sessions I can sense the energy he is exerting, which I then forward on to the clients.

My Indian guide is someone that I kept on seeing many years ago – I just continued to have this vision of a young Red Indian warrior with a rifle and a rack of bullets strapped across his chest. I could see him crystal clear, but I wanted to find out more details about him, and many times asked him: "What is your name, my friend?" But he would only reply: "My name is not important. It's the messages that I can send and the work that I want to do with you that is important." I know patience is a virtue, but it isn't one of my strong points, and I gave up on asking him in the end. If the spirits don't want to tell you something, they won't, it doesn't matter how many times you ask. I just put the question out of my mind for several years, but then one day he just came through to me and I could see him standing on a boulder. "My name is Proudfoot," he said, completely out of the blue. Maybe he was just trying to teach me a lesson to be more patient! He did tell me the name of his tribe, and showed me a picture of his squaw carrying a baby on her back; but apart from that I know nothing else about him – and obviously that's the way he wants to keep the relationship.

I have never put any questions to my Indian spirit about the after-life or indeed previous lives, I just feel his presence and energy. I know some mediums say they get huge amounts of information from their Indian guides, but I suppose it is not a side of spiritualism that interests me. One of my nieces once went for a regression session, although I advised her against it, and she came back rather distressed. She was told by the medium that in a former life she had gone through some very hard times as a peasant woman, and she found the whole experience quite upsetting.

I know many people have had satisfactory regression readings, although when I hear tales about how they were supposed to have been Mark Anthony or Cleopatra in a past life I just have to laugh. But I am not knocking all mediums who do this kind of work, it's just my personal stance. I have such a volume of work doing what I do, with so much of my time taken up by people who want me for purely spiritual messages and healing. I feel this is my calling, and I have never been interested in delving into past lives.

But I do believe in the Book of Life or the Akashic Records as they are referred to by spiritualists; many mediums will testify this is the complete ethereal record of all human thoughts and actions, which trained mediums can access if they have learned to attune their subconscious mind to the right wavelength.

15 – Belief in a God-force

A LEAFY BANK

Beneath a leafy bank ran a babbling brook,
all this was put there for man to see
the beauty which abounds.
The coursing river, the birds that sing,
these are all God's sounds

Put there so man can see nature at its best,
the beauty, the peace and tranquillity.
This beauty is put ehere for all time
so man can unveil the mystery of life
and make it all rhyme.

So be still, lay beside the brook,
be peaceful and serene,
only then can you take a look.

There are probably as many different versions of "God" and "Heaven" as there are mediums. Sylvia Browne has very strong religious beliefs and has even founded her own church, but I find some of her views bewildering – such as everyone in the spirit world being aged 30, whatever age they are when they leave this world. That is not the picture of after-life that I have been led to believe, in fact I find some of her views just ridiculous. Granted she has a big following, and she is a bit wacky, but the Yanks love all that don't they!

Although the basic general message from mediums about the next world may be similar, the detailed beliefs are sometimes very different. Maybe that adds strength to the cynics, but people must trust us as they find us – I know Sylvia has related many good success stories on the Montel Williams TV show, while many people have thanked me for messages that have proved accurate following disappointing readings with other mediums. How can this be explained? I wouldn't know where to start, I just know that time after time the spirits use me to pass on messages that mean something to somebody.

I can't say I have been on the receiving end of any specific spiritual messages that have had a dramatic effect on me, although I know many people have – for instance, Tony Stockwell reckoned he was saved from a car crash by one such message. However, I do continually ask for guidance regarding my personal pathway, and in fact my father's spirit must be quite fed up with my questions by now, many of them concerning my writing, which – apart from my readings with clients – is the main subject that has absorbed me over the last few months.

Some mediums do have really outlandish ideas though. Sometimes I have read their books and said to myself, what planet is that person on? If I come across some spiel that I think is so wide of the mark that it strikes me as preposterous, then I just close up the book and get on with my "work" as I see it. I do agree with Sylvia on one point – that the spirit guides are different to angels in that they have experienced life as we know it on Earth. I believe the angels that look after us are beings of light, while the guides are the product of energy.

I also agree with Sylvia that our Earthly sleeping time is when the spirits are drawn close and take over the subconscious mind, with the dreaming mechanism kicking in. My take on how the mind works is that if you are distraught about something, then the guides will come in and try to unravel the dreams. I believe the guides, through the brain, are trying to unscramble the worrying aspects of your life. But besides the release of any troubles, dreams also have a predictive level – a subject I referred to in a previous chapter when I mentioned my dream sequence that featured Princess Diana.

One piece of apparatus I have read about, and wouldn't mind trying, is the "God Helmet", an invention of the Canadian scientist Michael Persinger. This experimental neurotheology piece of equipment is said to stimulate the brain with magnetic fields that have had a profound effect on many trialists; a good percentage reported having psychic experiences that usually included the presence of a holy figure. I must add that it didn't seem to work on the proclaimed atheist Prof Richard Dawkins, but then I would have been surprised if it had! However, I wouldn't write off the God Helmet as another piece of psychic junk, and I wouldn't mind betting that the medical profession is keeping a close eye on these experiments

I used to go to quite a few spiritual churches when I was learning more about my pathway, but I must admit some of them left a lot to be desired. I found that many of the churches I attended are too wrapped up in their dogma, too entrenched in the past and don't really have time for "new age" people and ideas. Some are now trying to get away from a church image and are calling themselves Centres, which I suppose is one way to attract people who are not of a religious persuasion and may be put off by a church building. But it is no good going to a spiritualist church hoping to have the whole pathway ahead laid out in front of you, because these groups deal only in evidence of the present and the past; they do not dabble in fortune-telling or predicting the future in any way.

Some of the biggest hypocrites I have ever come across have been churchgoers, so I thought if that is the attitude of their religion I want nothing to do with it. I am not the sort of person who believes in going to church to pray en masse, that has not been the path for me, although I still believe we are guided by a higher force or power – call it God if you want. The way I dealt with the situation was to take the knowledge I felt I needed and disregard the rest, sorting out the wheat from the chaff so to speak. For instance, in one church the medium said to a fellow learner: "You like cornflakes for your breakfast, don't you." She told another: "The spirits are telling me you like fish and chips for your dinner," and to a third – on a boiling hot day – "You have been eating a lot of ice-cream." I can't believe God and the spirit world would want to insult people's intelligence with messages like that.

As I have said, I have never been a religious person, and in fact I suppose I followed the guidelines laid down by my parents – a bit like someone being biased towards a political party because that's the way their parents always voted. In a large family like mine, the only religion practised was: If you can't do a good turn for someone, don't do a wrong one. It was the philosophy of my mum and dad on life, and although they sent my sister and I to Sunday school, we knew it was just to get us out of the way and earn an hour or so of peace for themselves. And who could blame them with such a large family!

But I definitely believe there is a God-force of some kind that guides us all, and I do offer up pleadings and requests during healing sessions. Any thoughts that are sent up in this manner are prayers, in effect, but whether they go to the same God referred to by people in the orthodox churches, who am I to say? Another link between the Bible and the psychic world, I believe, is that the disciples of Jesus were mediums of a sort; they might have been fishermen, tax collectors and so on by vocation, but if the stories are to be taken seriously I feel they definitely had some kind of visionary gift – besides the sheer magnetism of the man they followed – that induced them to redefine their lives. One of my poems is entitled "God's Earth", but that did not come directly from me; that was channelled through Automatic Writing and obviously came from someone who was quite religious.

I've got my own beliefs. I'm a spiritualist, not a religious person – which is a personal choice I hear more and more these days, and it was interesting to hear singer Dolly Parton use exactly that same phrase to describe herself during one interview, although she was brought up in a large church-going family. In fact I would describe myself as a universalist, because I worry about the planet, about Mother Earth, the people and the animals. I did feel the warmth from one of the ancient "circle" stones at Avebury, but I don't go in for tree hugging. I think you have to let common sense prevail in some matters, so I wouldn't go as far as Prince Charles in talking to plants and trees. But I do love that being-close-to-nature feeling, just sitting on a lawn or under a tree, gaining inspiration from Mother Nature, especially in parks that have water features and country areas with babbling brooks. And the first time I visited a Wiltshire arboretum I was quite overcome by the sheer beauty of the floodlit trees and shrubs.

When it comes to dealing with people, I would never do anybody down and would never do anything knowingly bad to anyone – that's the religion I inherited from my parents. The humanist outlook also came from my dad, who was the kind of person who would never do any wrong to anyone. So I think we were brought up the right way without religion being thrust down our throats.

You may find this surprising, but I have had many religious people come to me for readings – including a nun who wanted some advice on her future pathway. This sister of mercy was thinking of calling it a day with her Order and wanted some guidance, but I'm afraid I can't say whether the messages I gave her swayed her one way or the other.

I have also had some people of strong Catholic faith come to see me, which surprised me because I didn't think Vatican followers believed in the work of mediums. I never fail to be amazed by the people from all walks of life who do come for a consultation.

16 – It's Not Hypnotism

A PIANO

A piano stood, playing out its favourite tunes,
sounding very grand.
It was playing by the light of the silvery moon,
and take me back to the promised land.

Everyone singing along, feeling very jolly,
if only we could let ourselves go
we could reach such dizzy heights,
We could let our hearts ring out
and let our souls take flight.

Sing, sing, over again,
sing, sing out aloud.
Just let go of your soul,
come on now, don't be proud.

I know some mediums have summoned up powers that transmit over the telephone wires. They are able to give a spiritual reading over the phone – and it is something I have done. Maybe not with the success of Edgar Cayce, whom I have already mentioned, but then he was a rather special person.

Although many people have said my voice has a very soothing quality, the telephone reading is not a method that I am at ease with. One lady said to me: "I was creeping up the wall before I phoned you, I was so tense. But listening to you has had a real calming influence. I feel so much better."

So it doesn't always have to be a hands-on experience or a face-to-face confrontation, but to be honest I just prefer to have a one-to-one situation. Some people may feel it is a cop-out, but the truth is that I simply feel more comfortable dealing with people when I am in my own surroundings in my own home, and naturally that makes for better working conditions. When there is distance between me and a client I find it quite impersonal, and I need to connect with a person's aura and energy field.

Many mediums have also had success at divining, or dowsing as it is known – the art of finding water or materials through the use of divining rods. I'm sure we've all seen film of people holding a forked twig that goes berserk at a certain point; some people even use an old metal coathanger and get the same result.

I've tried it with a pendulum, and it doesn't work for me, but I have had success with the rods. On one occasion a lady wanted me to find a well that she had been told was once in use in her garden. My rods indicated a spot where a tree now stood, and a bit of back-breaking digging proved I was right.

My experience with the pendulum proves that we can't all be good at everything; I just didn't have an affinity with it. But I have no trouble finding energy sources using the rods.

One subject in which I never get involved, however, is hypnotism. I have already tried to explain the art of relaxation and a self-trance, but I wouldn't let anyone else put me into a trance. I think I have a fear of losing my gift through it.

I know people like Paul McKenna have made a career out of hypnotising people, and I cannot deny that what he and many other people do in that field can be very entertaining. But as far as I'm concerned, that's what it is – part of the entertainment world, and I am not interested. Not only do I not like the idea of another person controlling my mind, but I also would not want to be made a fool of – and you can't tell me that some of those hypnotism acts don't do that. Being taken up on stage and acting out the movements of a concert pianist, or being given a pen and told it is a broom with which to sweep the floor, may sound like fun to some people but please leave me out of it. And despite what these practising "entertainers" might claim about the innocence of their acts, there have been documented cases of people suffering depression after being hypnotised.

I also never get involved in past-life regression. My take on life is that I have a job keeping up with the work that I am being sent in this lifetime, without dealing with the past and wondering who I might have been in a previous life.

People might think that bringing on a self-induced trance is akin to being hypnotised, but I can assure there is a big difference. When I meditate to a trance state it is something I am doing for myself, not letting someone else take charge of my mind and actions. What I am doing is letting the spirit guides use me as a medium. And when I have been in a group of like-minded people we make sure the doors are locked and the phone is off the hook – it is a controlled atmosphere. Something like a ringing telephone or a noise interruption can shock a person out of a trance, but being brought back in that manner is not good for the body and it can take a while for the recovery. My first out-of-body experience, for instance, really made me feel quite spaced out because I think I came back too quickly, and it took a couple of days to recover.

A lot has been written about star signs, and they continue to take up acres of space in some popular newspapers and magazines. I do believe there may be something in the astrological charts if a person's exact time of birth is known; that is more of a science. But as far as I'm concerned the magazine horoscope columns and plethora of telephone services now available are far too general to be taken seriously; they are good entertainment and should be treated as such.

I've already said I don't touch the Tarot cards either, and that goes for Angel cards or Mermaid cards or what other fancy name some fortunetellers give them. To my mind, a pack of cards could give one reading one day and a completely different outlook on another day. But it is a fact that people do get hooked on them – I knew one woman who was laying out the cards several times a day, even before breakfast. That's obsession, and it cannot be healthy.

One woman came to me after receiving a Tarot reading, but I had to tell her that when her guides linked up with me they were not sending out the same message as the cards about her relationship at the time. The woman, who was about 30 years old and a mother of three little girls, obviously didn't want to believe me and the meeting became quite confrontational.

I said: "I can't give you the answer you want to hear if I am receiving a different message. I am definitely not picking up the name given to you by the Tarot reader, that's the way it is coming through. I am a medium – on a higher level than Tarot."

The image I saw was of a man running away, his shoes kicking up a cloud of dust, and I knew she would not be able to pin him down. I told her: "Go home and put the relationship to the test if you have 100 per cent faith in him. Ask him outright if he wants to stay with you."

Some time later she came back to me, and immediately was apologetic about her attitude at our first meeting. Apparently the man told her he did want her, but could not take on the three girls – which obviously came as part of the package. They went their separate ways, but the story had a happy ending because she said she was now in a new relationship that was going very well.

Another of my clients admitted he had been to a Tarot "expert" who had merely read him extracts from a book. Would you pay money for that?

I used to attend psychic fairs, but that was mainly during my learning years; it is not something I do these days on a regular basis. It was fine seeing other mediums in action as part of the learning curve, but dealing with members of the public in that kind of atmosphere is again not something I feel comfortable with. For a start, these kind of events are usually quite noisy, and I cannot concentrate properly in a setting like that. It may be OK for Tarot readers, but when I go to psychic fairs these days it is really just to see how NOT to do it!

I listened in on a Tarot reader one day, with a client sitting on the edge of his seat lapping up every word – but the messages he was getting were not the ones he should have got, not according to what my tuned-in antenna was telling me. Afterwards I said to her: "How long have you been reading the cards?" She said: "About six months." Well, no wonder the poor man went away with his head full of nonsense ideas – to my mind you need far longer than six months to develop and gain the experience for proper readings, and I'll argue that with anyone. I came across a young man leading a ghost-busting exercise not too long ago; he was aged about 20 but talked as if he knew all there was to know about the spiritual world. How can he know it all at that age? I know they have to start somewhere, and we do need more young people to become good mediums, but some of them have learned a little and get carried away by their own bravado.

It is also my belief that a lot of mediums conducting sessions in churches don't have the necessary experience or skills to do the job. And many others have been stuck in the same environment for too long – they haven't moved on and their dogma is the same as it was yonks ago. Many spiritualist churches are changing their names to spiritual centres to try and get away from the religious stigma, but I feel they still need personnel changes if they are to survive.

Some years ago I did a couple of stage shows, the sort that people like Gordon Smith and Tony Stockwell are renowned for doing around the country. But again I don't feel it's the best forum for my skills and I'm not comfortable with it. It's not a question of sour grapes, because I think my events were quite successful. I feel it's too easy to give messages to the wrong people in a large gathering – I've witnessed it quite a lot. In fact I know at one meeting the message was for me (it included my love of rock'n'roll, amongst other things), but it went to the woman sitting in front of me. Needless to say, I kept quiet and just used the experience as an observer.

I don't sit easily with the stage show process; I feel a bigger responsibility. The only occasion I would do something like that now is if I was at a small spiritual gathering where the medium failed to turn up; it has happened, and I have been asked to step in.

But from a personal point of view, I would rather work on a one-to-one basis, or at the most one-to-two. Even with two people it can sometimes become a little muddled as to who the message is for, so imagine how tangled it can be for the spirits dealing with a room full of people.

Now when it comes to lecturing, that's different. I don't mind giving my views to a group because I can prepare the content and I know I have the experience to deal with a question-and-answer session at the end. For me, it's a case of staying mainly in my comfort zone and continuing to do what I do best.

17 – Coincidence or What?

One facet of spiritualism unfortunately makes the medium the butt of quite a few jokes. I expect everyone has experienced some kind of telepathy, where a person's name or face comes into the mind for no apparent reason, and then the phone rings and that person is on the other end of the line. Well, imagine that happening on a very regular basis.

That is what happens to me. I'll pick up the phone and say: "Hello Joy," and Joy will say: "How did you know it was me?" I must add that I haven't got one of those fancy modern phones that shows the number or name of the caller, and it's not clairvoyance. It's just telepathy, and I'm afraid it reveals itself in mediums more than the average person because we are able to tune in to extra energies and thoughts. But we have to put up with a lot of jokes along the lines of: "I expect you knew it was me knocking at the door," or "I bet you knew I would ring you today." And quite often I do know.

One lady I had never before had contact with was ringing for an appointment recently and, I don't know what made me say this but, as I was making a note in my diary I said: "That will be Carly, then." She said: "That's spooky, how did you know my name?" There was another occasion when I met a client at the door, and I did know her name. I knew it wasn't Sylvia, but I found myself saying: "Come on in, Sylvia." She said: "Why did you call me that. In fact it's my mother's name."

I can't always explain what happens when I open my mouth. The spirits no doubt have their own explanation. "Déjà vu" experiences of life happen at times to everybody, I know that, and usually we just put it down to coincidence or a trick of the memory. But weird things seem to happen to me too often to just write them off as an accident, chance or a twist of fate. For instance, I was out shopping the other week and bumped into a friend called Wendy who I hadn't seen for at least five years. After I left her I went into another store and met someone called Alan who I also hadn't seen for many years. Now, Wendy's husband, who passed away some time ago, was called Alan. Was that all a series of acts called coincidence, or were the spirits at work trying to point my mind in a certain direction?

That is just one little example, but sometimes the turn of events are just too weird to always call it coincidence, especially, as I say, when they seem to happen on a very regular basis. For instance, I went through a phase shortly after I began my writing when the same people seemed to keep popping up in my life, and I didn't know why. But I do believe there are reasons for this behaviour and putting it down to coincidence is just too simplistic.

Many mediums believe in synchronisation, that the order of events in our lives is not coincidental at all but is in fact governed by a higher authority. For the time being I'll stick to the "weird" definition, although I do think Wendy popped back into my life for a good reason.

Sometimes I just feel I have been put in the right place at the right time. For instance, one day I was again in my local supermarket – it's a fairly small place and so obviously I know most of the staff quite well – and one of the young lads came up to me in quite an upset state. We just seemed to collide, but I began to link with him straight away. He said he was living in a hostel and feeling quite down; however, I was able to tell him he would be getting engaged, that he would play a father-figure role, and also that he would be getting an offer on a house and would be moving quite soon. This was such an unusual scenario for me – I don't normally start giving life-line readings to people I bump into while out shopping; but for some reason I had linked immediately with the spirit of this boy's father.

Two weeks later I met the lad's mother. "I have to thank you for what you said to my son," she said. "We were really worried about his state of mind, but he came home full of the joys of spring after talking to you."

I then met the boy again shortly afterwards and he told me he had an interview for a place to live the next day. I went home and meditated, asking his father to help – and would you believe it, within a day or two I met his son in the street again and he planted a big kiss on my cheek. He had moved into his new home, and the smile on his face was priceless. "This is your new beginning, don't mess up," I told him. I'm sure the engagement followed – I have faith in the spirit guides.

Psychometry is something different. According to my dictionary it is about the relative strength of mental faculties, but in my language it is the energy stored in objects which is able to be detected even after long periods of time. Just as our fingerprints cannot be easily erased, so the energy remains from objects that we have worn and touched. Material things left behind by people who have passed over have a lot of data on them, and places reveal complex energy fields.

When John and Jane came to see me, John took out a ring and placed it on the table. "What do you make of that," he said. To be honest, I thought it was a rather ugly ring, one that had been found buried in his father's garden. I picked it up, but swiftly put it down again – it had bad vibes and made my head swim. I didn't like the look or feel of it. I could tell it was a hand-made ring of yesteryear, made by a smithy because the joints were visible, and with a big, nasty, brown stone. It was obviously a man's ring, and as I tuned in to it I could tell it once belonged to a monk, one who was higher up the order – in fact the ring was the same colour as a monk's habit. I just felt there was something sinister about it and handed it back as quickly as possible.

But I did say I would try and find out more about its origins, and while I was flicking through history books at the library – without any rhyme or reason – a book just fell into my hands. It was a book about the War of the Roses, the 15th century battle between the Yorkshire and Lancashire districts. When I told John what had happened he went a whiter shade of pale. He said, "You could not have known, but my surname is Lancaster." I was as astounded as him – why should that particular book fall off the shelf?

I have already explained that I never ask for a person's surname when they book a reading, and if they tell me I quickly forget it anyway; I'm just not into surnames because I believe it keeps the relationship more private between a medium and a client. Going back to the ring, its history remains unknown; it was dug out of soil, but it definitely had a history all of its own.

Another experience was when I visited Wells Cathedral with a friend and found it a lovely old building, full of history. I was happy simply walking round, looking at the pictures and sculptures, reading about the various individuals associated with the place, when all of a sudden we came upon a little crypt. It was boxed off, and you had to go up a few steps to access it – but when I tried to climb them I began to feel faint. "I can't go in there, it makes me feel ill," I said. But I was intrigued as to the cause of this effect.

Urging my friend on, I said: "You go and see who is buried here," and he reported back that there was a fallen warrior with a long sword by his side. Apparently it was the burial place of a warlord who had fallen in battle, having died by the sword. I was obviously picking up bad vibrations, for these energies are still around from a few hundred years ago and can react on sensitive people.

Feeling energies is far removed from actually seeing them at work, however. And while some mediums claim to be able to instigate kinetic energy – moving articles by the power of the mind alone – all the experiments in which I have participated have ended in disappointment. I have already mentioned the *Men Who Stare at Goats* film, based on Governmental efforts to harness the power of psychics; and although John Travolta managed to do it in the film *Phenomenon*, when some bright light in the sky gave him telekinetic powers, that is Hollywood for you.

Coming down to reality, I have focused very strongly on an article and failed to move it, and I've also been in groups (fully believing that several mediums together can create a powerful force) that have attempted to call on this energy, without even a hint of success. I've heard mediums boast that they can do it, but it's one of those things that needs more than a leap of faith as far as I am concerned. I would need to see it to believe it, and so far it hasn't happened before my very eyes.

The experience known as PSP (Prescient Synchronicity Phenomenon) is another of those strange happenings that many people can relate to. They feel a physical pain for some unknown reason, but learn later that at that precise time something unpleasant happened to a loved one or dear friend.

You don't have to be psychic for that to happen. But what I often experience is a pain when I am giving a reading to a person who has an ailment, especially a cancer. I may get backache or pain in a leg – but it is the knowledge of that pain rather than the physical pain itself, although sometimes I can hardly breathe because of the intensity of the reading.

One of the worst attacks I suffered was a real PSP experience. I was in my bedroom when I suffered a feeling of choking – I really thought I was going to die; it was some time before I could get my breath properly and lift myself off the bed. The next day my partner at the time rang to say his mother had passed away, and the time of death was the exact time of my choking attack.

I also began to get messages through my automatic writing that my partner's father was about to leave this Earth very shortly, and that it would not be very long before I would be sitting in the church for his funeral. I sent the thought up to my guides: "OK, I got the message when his wife died, and I experienced the pain, so please don't do that to me again." Sure enough, the father passed away a few weeks later, but fortunately the spirits were kinder to me on that occasion and I didn't suffer physically.

18 – A Scary Experience

As I have said before, I don't mind seeing sceptics, in fact I welcome them because they are free-thinking individuals ready to question what they do not understand – and let's face it, seeing is not always believing, as Derren Brown has proved on television! You cannot see electricity, but you can prove it is there. And there are many more mysteries still to be explained on this Earth.

However, mediums are now becoming more accepted as a part of life – opening up the after-life. I see adults from all walks of life and of all ages, and it never ceases to make me chuckle to myself when someone says: "It won't be too frightening, will it?" It takes me back to when I was a teenager and had my first brush with a medium, and yes, I was a little nervous and scared myself at that time, so I fully understand.

Although the work of mediums and spiritualists is often featured and discussed on radio and television, even in these enlightened days there is still an air of mysticism about people who contact the spirit world. I can certainly understand a fear of the unknown, but what I cannot really understand is how mediums are still associated with witchcraft in some people's eyes, because personally I won't have anything to do with that side of things. I did see the film *The Exorcist* many years ago, which was supposed to be based on a factual psychic experience, and I must admit that the way it was presented even scared me a little. I was tempted to see the latest demonic offering, *Paranormal Activity*, which has been described as one of the most chilling films ever made, but in the end decided I would leave these aspects of Hollywood mind-play to those who want a hair-raising cinema experience and stick with the strands of the psychic world that I am comfortable with.

But it is a fact that the medium is still a scary figure to many people. For instance, when a client called Brian came for a reading recently he also made a booking for his friend Jim. "But don't be surprised if he doesn't turn up. He's scared to death of you," he said. In fact he did turn up, and I later heard reports about how he excitedly played the tape of the reading to other family members and told them he was keen to come for further sessions. That's what I call a success.

One recent visitor was a girl who walked in like a plank of wood, she was so stiff it was almost unbelievable. I tell people who are wary and sitting on the edge of their seat to relax and "drop down" or they will block the path for the spirits. If there is too much nervous tension I cannot work, and nor can the spirits. The funny thing was, when this girl left she said: "Oh my goodness, you are so normal! So down to earth." I'll take that as a compliment then.

Another man admitted he had been almost too scared to see me, but we had a brilliant reading and he said at the end: "I'm ever so glad I came." His wife had passed away less than a year previously, and she quickly came through for him. I picked up on the fact that their anniversary was soon coming up, and along with a few other messages it reduced him to tears. But he shook my hand at the door and was obviously in a lot better frame of mind than when he arrived.

When clients leave after meeting me for the first time they usually say: "That was really interesting. It wasn't what I had imagined." I never want to frighten anyone, I just set out to help people discover truth and inspiration, and sincerely hope that my thoughts through this writing will plant more seeds in people's minds so that they can investigate the spirit world for themselves.

However, there is a difference between a sceptic and someone who is utterly rude and unwilling to accept anyone else's opinion. Recently a lady came to me who had lost a daughter, and I was able to pick up on the spirit message and describe one of her daughter's favourite settings and even her mannerisms. I saw her sitting on a bench, smoking away despite the fact she had been warned it would affect her health; she crossed her legs in a quick, defiant manner. The mother said: "That is exactly how she was; she wouldn't be told." But the father, who was also in on the sitting, continually opposed his wife and repeatedly made his anger felt – to the point where I almost aborted the session. The man's attitude was so negative that it was surprising I was able to concentrate enough for anything to come through. Now, I can understand a parent's anger when one of their offspring dies before them, even though in this case she was no youngster; but to continue to direct that anger at other members of the family, neighbours and anyone else who happens to cross their path, is not a healthy frame of mind. It certainly doesn't lend itself to the kind of spiritual comfort that I am trying to help people achieve.

I cannot dispute the fact that despite all the television coverage these days, many people are still wary of meeting a medium and reticent about coming forward with their reasons for the visit. After a recent reading with a mother and daughter, who had travelled down from the north of England to see me, I asked if there was anything else they wanted to know. The mother eventually admitted they were hoping one certain person would come through, but they were disappointed.

I said: "Just give me a minute to try and connect." Then I had contact from a young spirit, my carpet began to look as if it was covered in snow, I started to feel freezing and my head hurt. We had all the heaters on in the room, but I felt the temperature drop and the mother exclaimed: "What's happening? It's gone stone cold in here." I could also see a tree, and got the impression he had been in a collision with this. He was telling me he had passed away instantly, and I relayed his message: "No life support, no hospital. Accident. Accident."

The mother was in tears. "He was just 20 years old. Thank you so much for that." She said her son was a young squaddie travelling back to his barracks during a period of winter snow and ice, and she was having nightmares about him suffering all alone when he passed over. I was able to reassure her that wasn't the case, but how tragic that a young man aiming to fight for his Queen and country should have his life cut short on a country road – there is no justice in that. But he did convey to us the fact that it was freezing cold on the night he died, and it never ceases to amaze me that these temperature changes are transmitted to the Earth plane.

The young man's spirit was literally throwing one or two things at me, and a reflex action made me duck out of the way. I relayed a couple of things that brought a laugh from the mother. "That's definitely him. He was a bit of a joker," she said. And I was able to draw comfort from the fact that the family took heart from hearing he was not alone in death and didn't suffer, otherwise it could have haunted them for the rest of their lives.

On her next visit, the mother said: "Can I ask a question?" I said that sometimes the spirits will answer a question, but other times the only information I get is what is volunteered. You can never tell. She said: "Ask what is going to happen to me in the coming year." And when I did, I had to duck from a bouquet of roses that was thrown at me. "My mother will get married next year, and tell her he is a diamond geezer," was the message I received.

The lady said she could see her son's face for a brief second or two, and that the phrase "diamond geezer" – which is not one I would ever use – was definitely her son speaking. And she confirmed: "It's true, I am getting married, and he is a very nice man."

She burst out crying at the evidence that the squaddie's spirit was still around his mother, and the fact that he was well aware of her pathway. The amazing sequel to this was when other members of the family later came for a reading – but had not told me they were related. I was confused at first when the same young soldier came through, giving me the feeling that he had become one of my regular spirit guides. But in fact he was there to give guidance and reassurance to other relatives, including one younger cousin who is hoping to become a professional footballer. It's another case of "watch this space" as the messages received were very positive.

Very often during a reading I'm the one who gets a shock. For instance, when I was in the midst of a session with a young girl aged about 20 I suddenly saw in front of us on the carpet a vision of a black Bible with a gold cross on the cover – the good old-fashioned sort of Bible with gold leaves on the front. I said, "Can you take a black bible," and she replied: "Yes, right on the back of the head!"

We both burst out laughing. Then she explained that the previous night she was looking for her grandmother's bible. She said: "My gran left it to me, and I said to myself, 'Alright Gran, if you are so clever, give me proof that you are around'. I was surrounded by tall bookcases and, as I bent down to put my slippers on, the Bible fell off one of the shelves and hit me on the head."

I said to her: "Well, if you wanted proof, you seem to have had it."

As I have said, I am not immune to shocks myself. One of the biggest I have encountered occurred just recently, when I thought I had finished my story and we were getting ready to publish. I received a telephone call telling me my sister Pat – who I knew was in hospital for an operation – had suffered a setback and was on a life-support machine. The strange thing is, just three days previously my father had made an appearance in my lounge, coming through to me as clear as any living person. He was holding out his hands and saying just one word, which at first I thought was "Ted", then I realised it was "dead", and he repeated it three more times. Then he was gone, as quickly as he had appeared.

When I received the news about Pat I dashed down to Cornwall as fast as I could. I knew she had been unwell for some time and had been in pain, although we all thought the operation was routine and that she would recover. When I entered the room where she was lying, I tried immediately to communicate with her telepathically, but who should I see standing beside her bed – none other than the spirit of my father again! I asked him if he was coming to take Pat on her journey to the Other Side, and he outstretched his hands to signify that he was. I felt her spirit leave and then come back into the room, as if she was asking for my permission to leave permanently. I felt I had to give it, to let her have the peace she wanted. My father was saying: "Look at her little finger, look at her little finger." I didn't know what he meant by this, but I reached under the covers for my sister's hand, and she moved her little finger. I knew then that she had heard my conversation, and understood that I had given my blessing.

A few days earlier she had related a dream she had about our mum, which had really startled her. She woke up saying: "Mother, mother, what are you doing here, what do you want?" That was obviously a precursor to what happened in the hospital. I had already had a premonition some 18 months previously that her death, when it happened, would be quite quick; it was something I had picked up during a session of Automatic Writing, and I remember telling my niece about it. And indeed she died the following lunch-time.

Now Pat wasn't a spiritual person, in fact she didn't really believe very much at all about what my life revolves around. She was one of those people who thought that when you die that's the end, simple as that. However, just three weeks after her death I was at a spiritualist meeting in Leicestershire being held by a young medium called Darren Brittain. I know people will think, after hearing about the work I do, that I should not be surprised at receiving any messages from the Other Side. But I can tell you, I could have been knocked over by a feather when Darren said my sister Pat was coming through for me. He was quick to verify who she was by naming one of her sons, and the message he relayed was that she was fed up with the pain on Earth and wanted her passing to be quick. Pat was just 65, which is by no means considered old these days.

19 – Death and Other Questions

IN BLUEBELL VALLEY

In bluebell valley there is a carpet of blue,
in bluebell valley there is a velvety hue.
This is what man cannot see,
the wonder that is there for you and for me.

These wonders go unseen, untouched,
yes my friends, we miss so much.
There is so much to gain as you stop to look and see
the wonders that are there for you and for me.

Man should take time to stand and stare,
to show the world he really has a care.
The land that abounds with gifts anew
have all been put there by God for me and you.

The rat race will still be there when you have gone,
so stop, my friends, to ponder on.

The subject of Death is naturally one of the most common to be discussed between a medium and a client. Many people want to know how death is described by the spirits, but the truth is there is no "death" as far as the spirit world is concerned; it's not a word that is used. I look on it as a transition.

One medium said to me a while ago during a philosophical conversation: "How do we know that we actually belong here, that we are not just here on a visit; that we are not already in spirit?" My answer is that we don't know; we are just on a journey, temporary residents on a sojourn. I believe we are here on the Earth plane to learn and evolve our own spirits. That is why we see and experience good things as well as bad – if we didn't, how would we be able to differentiate and equate? Once we go back to the spirit form our duties are to act as guides, that is what I am led to believe.

Why can't the spirits give us a clearer view of Heaven, or whatever you want to call the Other Side? That's another favourite question, and my answer is that the spirits that come to me are not all-seeing, all-knowing souls, they are merely the descendants of Joe Public, everyday people in the main.

My belief is that after death the body goes into a state of collective consciousness and passes into the Akashic records – also known as the Book of Life, like a giant computer for the spiritual world – and that is what mediums are able to tap into. I go there because that's where all the wisdom and knowledge is for our present lives and the future; I am just not interested in regression into past lives. I just think certain people have this gift of being able to access these files, and I am lucky enough to be one of them.

I would say the most-asked question from clients concerns their relatives' state of mind in their final stages of this life. "When someone is on a life-support machine or in a coma, can they hear you?" is what many people want to know. I say they can, because the audio system is the last part of the human brain to close down.

Can unborn babies hear? Again I am sure they can. One young mother told me that during her pregnancy she would often lay with a small transistor radio on her stomach, believing it might transfer relaxing vibes to her womb. When the child was three years old, one breakfast time she suddenly came out with: "Mummy, when I was in your tummy I really liked that music you used to play to me." The woman said she was dumbstruck and nearly dropped the teapot she was holding at the time. For the fact that she held the radio on her bump was something that she never confided in anyone, not even her husband.

So if a foetus can pick up vibrations from a radio, I think the same sort of thing happens to people on life-support machines. And I have had so much evidence over the years from all sorts of people that it does happen.

Another question I am often asked is how do I know the spirit world is a happy place? Well, all I can tell you is that in my experience the spirits are generally in a happy state of mind. I know I am dealing with bereavement and very serious subjects much of the time, and usually I will admit the spirits are on a purely guidance level, but there have been occasions when the vibrations have been right up to the ceiling and the client and I have been howling with laughter, the tears rolling down our cheeks.

Not all readings are about doom and gloom. One that went well was when a young lady received messages from the grandad she adored. He revealed a great sense of humour, and the girl said that was exactly what he was like – a clown prince, loved by all the family. "You have got him down to a T. He was a real comedian, always making us laugh, and I can see he hasn't changed."

I said: "Why is he showing me a set of toy false teeth, the sort you wind up with a key to make them chatter and move around?" She said he didn't have a tooth in his head. Then I said: "Why is he now showing me toffee, stretching it from arm to arm?" She laughed until she cried, saying: "He loved toffee, but because he had no teeth he had to gum it to death." We both fell about laughing. "That was my grandad exactly. I wouldn't have missed this for the world," she said as she left. He was a lovely man, and there was a high energy around him; people like that seem to come back with the same personality they had on Earth. It was the kind of reading that is so uplifting to me as well as the client.

I also believe there are pleasurable things like music still to be enjoyed when we leave this world – I have often heard the spirits singing, so the Andrew Lloyd Webbers and musicians of this world can definitely have something to look forward to. One woman client of mine was putting over such a stubborn attitude that I distinctly heard the Frank Sinatra song *My Way* coming over loud and clear; on other occasions I have heard *Happy Birthday* being sung to celebrate an Earth birthday.

But it's not always like that, and indeed some readings can be very stressful. I have had occasions where the client has sent a spirit on his way! I remember a reading I was doing for a Canadian lady, and I happen to link in with both her mother-in-law and father-in-law at the same time. When I told her, she said: "You can tell them to go away, I don't want to speak to them." I said: "You realise you have lost my guides. I am going to have to abort this reading I'm afraid." Her friend then followed her in and we had a brilliant session, with guides coming through freely and messages being well received. "Don't worry about my colleague," she told me, "she does the same thing at Tarot readings." You just have to accept that some people seem to enjoy being miserable and unco-operative. You can't win them all.

I know some mediums, like Sylvia Browne, describe a very detailed view of the after-life that includes theatres, sports events and the everyday pursuits such as fishing and gardening that most of us enjoy. But my idea of the spirit world is not so clear-cut; I believe we enter a collective consciousness of thought that is like a giant memory bank. There is definitely more to our lives than what we perceive on this Earth, but obviously many of the stories we read have been embellished and dramatised over the years so that it is difficult to understand what is myth, legend or the truth. Each person has to sort out the wheat from the chaff and try and stay "grounded", if that doesn't sound absurd for a world that is usually associated with being far above us in the sky!

Another question I am asked a lot is: Do I believe in reincarnation? It's a subject on which I keep a very open mind. I've read many books on the subject, but I'm still sitting on the fence on this one. It's a bit like extra-terrestrials as far as I'm concerned – I've never seen one, but that doesn't mean they don't exist.

Because I'm not that interested in regression, it doesn't mean I don't believe that we have past lives. I'm sure the Akashic Records do include a complete history that includes a blueprint of our present lives on Earth – all of our actions and thoughts, that's why we have the saying 'What goes around, comes around'. We may consist of skin, bone, masses of tissues and a heart, but we are still pure energy; sometimes we are able to access this, which results in us having a "gut feeling" about something.

I strongly believe our pathways are mapped out for us, and are written into our aural energy fields. It's just that I'm not personally interested in that side of spiritualism. The Records are about the collective thoughts that mediums tap into. So I don't disbelieve all the stories I hear about regression and reincarnation – in fact some of the evidence I have witnessed is very strong. Maybe one day I will get more involved in those topics, but at the moment my time is taken up with mediumship and healing, and I don't want to get sidetracked from this work.

Another favourite question is regarding soul mates – do we have one soul mate with whom we will spend eternity, or are there several? I know people like Rita Rogers, another very well-known medium who has written a complete book on the subject, believes everyone on this planet has just one soul mate with whom they were probably paired before they were born. She actually advises people as to whether they are with the right soul mate, but I don't ever want to get into that kind of reading. That's a big responsibility.

I am more inclined to agree with George Meek, the serious spiritual investigator I mentioned in a previous chapter. He described the "soul mate" theory as a dangerous concept after discovering that some people had been incited to move in with their designated "mate", even if it meant splitting up a marriage partnership and abandoning children. I believe that in this world you will read the books you are meant to read, you will visit places you are meant to visit, and you will meet people you are meant to meet. If it is meant to be, then your paths will cross.

Soul mates is not a subject I am happy writing about; it's the same with my lectures – I have to be fully confident I know what I am talking about before I tackle a subject. Knowledge or belief is where we all get the confidence factor from, isn't it, and I am no different to the next person.

To the pet lovers of this world, I can reassure them that there is a "heaven" for their favourite animals. During many readings I have had various pets coming through – cats, dogs, even horses – but only to show themselves. They walk around in a square in front of me, and I know from the form they take whether they are still alive or in the spirit world.

Some animals show their Earthly characteristics so clearly. One little dog had one ear up and one down – "That is exactly how he used to sit," said the owner.

When I was young one of our family pets was a tiny Yorkshire terrier called Tessa, which some people used to make fun of. "That's not a dog, that's a rat," they would say, but I loved her to bits. She wasn't big enough to jump up on my bed unaided, so I would pick her up and she would snuggle down with me. That dog had a lot of human attributes about her – she seemed to know what I was thinking sometimes, and what I was about to do; I guess many pet owners can relate to that kind of relationship. After she passed over I was lying in bed one night and felt her footsteps coming up the bed, and she dropped down beside me just like she used to. I sent out the thought: "I know you are there, Tess."

People who have never had pets don't quite understand the bonding between a human and an animal, but I am fully aware that pets are like children or close friends to so many of us. I have often described the shape or size of an animal that has passed over, and it can bring great comfort for the owner to know that the pet is happy in the after-life. Oh yes, animals definitely have spirits!

20 – Automatic Writing

THE SWAN

A swan floated on a pond, in all her majesty,
pure and white with her beautiful wings,
her webbed feet of yellow.

The more you look at this beautiful creature
the more you begin to mellow.

Feed her some bread, give her some corn,
stop to think why you were born.

A medium once told me I would one day write books, but of course I never believed her. Get yourself a life, I thought. I can't write; I don't even want to write. However, I now realise that if you turn "can't" into "can" – as one of my close friends once told me, it only means knocking off a T – then anything is possible. It was another of life's lessons I had to learn.

I began a phase of my life in which I couldn't stop writing. I couldn't pass a stationery shop without wanting to go inside and root around for what I call posh pens. Something different was happening to me; I was beginning to think more rationally than for a long time.

Something was guiding me – and it was the gift of Automatic Writing. When I sat down to write I always sent up a few prayers along the lines of: "Well, if you want me to write this book, do you mind coming down to help me, Amen." Then I could not seem to stop writing. I amazed myself, and when I read it back I could see the lessons I had learned.

The idea of a book was put into my mind at one of the first spiritual church sessions I ever attended. It was a meeting of mediums and would-be mediums, and the woman taking the meeting asked the spirits what role they wanted me to take. "Write a book" was the reply. However, one of the things I always thought implausible, even impossible, was writing a book. I had no interest in writing, and could not type, yet I have already published a small book of poems and for some time had the urge to put my experiences down on paper in the hope they would encourage other people who felt the same as me to develop their senses.

The verses and notes I have since made all came through Automatic Writing, a form of communication I have since used many times; I have put it to the test over and over again, and found it always comes up with the answers. Other mediums will know what I mean by Automatic Writing – the state of mind is called "lightly overshadowed", and the only way I can describe it is feeling as if I have had two or three glasses of wine. I'm not talking about going into a full trance, which is a state that most mediums enter through controlled breathing. No, my writing comes mostly through my personal pathway; if I have a question, then the pen seems to have a mind of its own and finds the answer. It is a technique I learned through meditation, which is something I have practised for many years and have now got down to a fine art.

One of the first times I tried it the name Barbara appeared in my notebook, but I was a little baffled because I didn't know anyone called Barbara. However, that same evening I was invited to a healing circle, and the first person to greet me gave me her personal card – she was called Barbara! I thought, this could be interesting, let's see where this leads. I believe we are all guided towards certain people and places, and this Barbara turned out to be a lovely lady; I didn't go looking for her, she just appeared in my life, and the evening turned out to be a success.

Like most people, I was originally sceptical of this form of writing, but found that by meditating enough and learning to open myself up completely, I was beginning to channel thoughts on to paper by tapping into this other energy field, shifting the mind back to allow the spirits to come through.

It was a hard slog to begin with, probably because of my original reluctance to accept my spiritual gift; and I wonder if this writing in later life is some sort of penance for skipping school lessons. It is ironic, because when I was a 14-year-old schoolgirl I hated typing, and can honestly say I didn't touch a typewriter for years after leaving school. Mind you, I hated just about every school lesson if the truth be known, which is why I sometimes played truant and would rather disappear into town to try out lipsticks and perfumes than sit in a boring old classroom. I wasn't a very good role model, but I now stand proud in the knowledge that I got there in the end.

And how did this return to the typewriter happen? It began with me hearing a version of Abba's song *I Had a Dream* at a Christmas carol service, and you know how it happens sometimes, you just hear a song and can't get it out of your mind. That tune haunted me and I couldn't stop singing it. It was while I was searching through tapes and records in a charity shop that I stumbled over something on the floor – it turned out to be a little old beaten-up manual typewriter. It looked like a museum piece, and I wasn't amused that it was left where people could trip over it. The friend who had accompanied me said: "My dad has got one at home just like that."

A week or two later that typewriter was still playing on my mind. I rang up my friend and said: "If your dad really has got an old type-writer, what are the chances of me borrowing it?" And so I came into possession of an old banger that had definitely seen better days and, with no irate teacher shouting at me, I soon learned how to get around the keyboard. One stiff back and a few broken nails later, I had mastered my new toy well enough to put down a few sentences. Then the next step was to borrow my daughter's electric typewriter, and being able to rub out and rectify mistakes was like manna from heaven.

The learning process may have been unconventional, but it worked for me. One inspiration was watching a documentary about children's writer Enid Blyton, who apparently typed out all her manuscripts using a single finger on some great big old-fash-ioned pre-war machine. I used to tell myself that if she could do it, so could I, and offered up my little prayers in the usual way. Devel-oping my state of meditation, the keyboard flashed away – no one-finger typing for me – and the words just continued to flow. If it's a mystery to you, then it remains an even bigger mystery to me! The only answer is that I was being guided, and in a funny sort of way it stopped being a pain and I actually started to enjoy the process; I stopped battling against my first reactions and, would you believe,

I even joined a literary class where I made a lot of new friends with writing skills. How did I find this class? Again it was being in the right place at the right time, like falling over a typewriter in a junk shop. Some people call it luck or chance, but I don't believe in that. I put it down to a combination of fate and guidance that changes a person's life.

So now when I'm sitting in my favourite park, notebook at the ready, I realise I'm writing – but I don't know what's been written until I read it through afterwards. I have been asked by people who have read my poems: "Are you not conscious of the wildlife around you, and the plants and various vegetation that you write about?" Well, of course I'm aware of the animals, insects and plant life that accompany us on this Earth, and I love to be surrounded by these things, but I have never consciously written about them. Some mornings I have been thinking about nothing in particular when the message comes into my head: "Pick up a pen." Then the poems and the prose appear through my handwriting.

It comes through with no punctuation, no full stops or anything, that's the way I feel obliged to write – it's a weird feeling; sometimes it takes me a while to make head or tail of it when I read it back and I think: "My god, where did I leave my brain?" It would be so nice to have hindsight before an event, but having my memories recounted in this manner is a lesson in itself. I always say the best teacher I have had in this life is life itself.

Another strange point is that the writing is often different from day to day – sometimes it slants one way, sometimes the other and sometimes it's fairly straight. I suppose it shows the thoughts come from different spirit guides. I'm sure most of them are coming from my father, because I recognise certain words and phrases he would have used, but not all of them.

One of the guides uses the words "thine" and "thee" a lot. They are words from way back when, words we don't normally use today; you find them in Biblical times but nowadays I think you would have to travel to rural parts of Yorkshire to hear those kind of words in everyday useage, and as far as I know I don't have any distant relatives from that part of the country.

The writing at first was more driven than inspired. "You have not got both hands on this writing project," I was told by more than one medium, and it was true. Every time I tried, I did a little and then the pages would go back into the cupboard and be forgotten for a while. "Give me some inspiration," I pleaded, and of course another medium would later give me a push to start again. Eventually I began to enjoy the experience, which has been an unexpected bonus for me. I never ever thought I would be writing poems or stories, real-life or fictional, but, believe it or not, it has all been through Automatic Writing.

After completing my first small book of poems, which still seemed like hard work, I began to aim my first autobiographical book firmly at the subject of adversity and how to overcome life's hurdles. I have learned so many things the hard way, not out of textbooks, and yet realise that many people have far worse things to cope with – such as terminal illness. I have come to the conclusion that we all have our crosses to bear, and that we must have certain burdens and suffering in order to know the difference between good and bad. "What did I do to deserve this heartache?" is a cry we have all probably resorted to at some time, but I can honestly say that now I am a lot older and wiser I no longer ask this question. I have found a belief and a philosophy for life which now makes a lot of sense; my pathway has made me a lot calmer and more caring about the planet and the people with whom I share this Earthly world. "Always have hope" is my main message to souls who are sick and troubled, because hope does spring eternal, and once you have snuffed out the light on hope then you could be forever floundering in the dark.

How is it that doctors and nurses manage to carry on their jobs, mainly in a cheerful mood, when all they see most of the time is grief, pain and the downside of people? The answer is that they have more dedication and hope than the norm, and have been hand-picked for this caring and inspiring profession.

Just spare a little time to sit down and recall the memories of your past; take stock of what you have achieved for yourself and for other people. It seems to me that the most unhappy people are those who appear to have everything, including an easy passage in life. You may envy the millionaires with their trappings of wealth, but the successful businessman I once worked for was prepared to step on anyone's toes to get what he wanted; a more insular man it would be hard to find, and in fact he was both feared and despised by a lot of people. It is human nature to want the best for yourself and your family, to have some creature comforts and be able to afford nice holidays. But you reap what you sow, and at the end of the day there is definitely a price to pay.

Several mediums have told me I have more than one book inside me, and I have long had an interest in books, usually searching out the old rather than the new. The information in many old books written by mediums is quite unlike the works produced by the modern writers, and has given me a great insight into the spirit world.

I used to seek out books on the subject in olde worlde junk shops, and was completely fascinated by people like Edgar Cayce, who has been described as "the world's greatest psychic", and with good reason. I don't think he wrote any books himself, but many have been written about him and are still available for psychic research. He was a very humble, not particularly well educated American who said he never read any book apart from The Bible, and in fact at one time refused to pursue his own psychic powers because they went against his religious beliefs. But fortunately he was persuaded to continue with both life and regressional readings, and thousands of recorded statements are still being studied at a special research centre set up in his name in Virginia.

What Cayce came out with, when in a self-induced trance (not hypnotised by anyone), was absolutely amazing and in a variety of languages; whether it was concerning personal pathway, healing, regression or missing persons. His wife would ask the questions and his secretary would take notes – hence the complete record for posterity. I would certainly recommend his works to anyone interested in taking a serious view of the psychic world.

However, I cannot agree with all Cayce's pronouncements, for while he believed anyone could do what he did, I still believe it's a gift that only a minority of people can tune in to and develop, and very few have taken it to the level that Edgar Cayce did. But in my early learning days, the more mustier the state of the book, the more it interested me. I found people like Helen Duncan, Arthur Findley and Arthur Conan Doyle to be fascinating role models.

Helen Duncan was a Scottish mother-of-six who practised as a materialisation medium in the first half of the 20th century and is famous for being the last person to be jailed under the antiquated Witchcraft Act during World War 2. This was after she revealed the name of a ship that had been sunk but was apparently still on the Government's "state secret" list.

Conan Doyle, famed for his Sherlock Holmes detective novels, is not generally so well known for his involvement as a spiritualist, but in fact became a very spiritual person after the death of his wife and son; in fact he was a prolific writer on many subjects, including *The History of Spiritualism* published in 1926. One of the fascinating aspects of some of his works is that they are believed to contain hidden clues about some of the major hoaxes of the day.

Whatever the truth, he was an intriguing character – as was the other Arthur, Mr Findlay, whose training college for mediumship and healing in Essex I once visited. A stockbroker and writer by profession, he helped to found the Psychic News and left his manor house home to the Spiritualists' National Union, which has continued to run the college. I must admit I still find it more interesting to read about people of that era rather than follow the mediums of today's television channels.

It was while browsing around one of my favourite secondhand bookshops some years ago that a very funny incident took place. It was the kind of place that is difficult to find nowadays – full of disorder, books piled from floor to ceiling, where you can spend all afternoon if you want to, just rummaging around.

Shortly before the visit a medium had told me: "I don't know why, but I'm getting this message to pass on to you: 'There'll be bluebirds over the white cliffs of Dover'. Does it mean anything to you?" I replied: "Absolutely nothing!" However, inside the bookshop I tripped over one of the many boxes strewn around, and put my hand on a pile of books to stop myself falling. I could hardly believe what I saw on the cover of the top book – a picture of three bluebirds! I leafed through it and discovered it was a book of poems, which I bought and took home. After I read it, I thought: "I wish I could write poems like that." And a couple of months later my first poems started to come through.

Who do I think is sending them? It is my father, who didn't write poetry himself as far as I know, but who was a very philosophical man and who told me at a very early age: "The pen is mightier than the sword." Some of my poems do seem to have a deep meaning, and they do contain the sort of phrases my father would have come out with.

I wrote a whole series of poems over a period of about a year. I didn't choose to write them, and in fact I found it rather hard work, worrying about why they were coming through and what I would do with them. My belief is that I was being shown this period of life here on Earth is not all there is. How can a three-year-old child play Mozart, or an autistic teenager produce drawings of an unbelievable quality? To my mind these things have no logical explanation; the answers come from another sphere.

It's another day, and here I am in my little park again. The fountain is going flat out, with the cascading water creating a wonderful sound that I find really inspiring. I have reached a point in my life where I am quite happy with my lot and nothing much fazes me.

When another medium told me I had the creation in my head for a book, and just needed to get my head down and concentrate, it gave me the kick-start I needed to continue with the project. I knew I would eventually receive help from my spirit friends to meet the right people, push on and complete the work.

Now a brass band has struck up in the park – I can't believe my luck, for military marches were my father's favourite music, and I gave him a set of four albums shortly before he passed away. I still have them, so although the conductor's baton brought sweet music indeed to my ears, I can't help feeling a bit tearful as the memories flood back.

I'm only sorry I didn't have this peace of mind in the first half of my life, but I suppose it comes down to the personal yardstick idea – if my whole life had been one long happy episode, how would I fully appreciate this current peaceful period and feel its true reward?

A swan on the pond reminds me of my first attempt at Automatic Writing – my little book of poems that has a picture of a swan on the front to represent peace and tranquillity.

Back in my favourite surroundings I recently began to encourage more Automatic Writing, and I was pleasantly surprised to find the responses were quite positive – regarding my private pathway as well as my aspirations to find a publisher.

I may have had success at Automatic Writing, but another facet of mediumship that some people can produce – and I haven't had much success at – is Psychic Art. And it's not for the want of trying. I know of mediums who have produced artwork that resembles a face or place, without ever having seen the original, and the reason I can confirm that this form of art is not merely a myth is because I have been the subject of such a painting. (Witness the front cover of this book!)

Some years ago this fantastic example came into my hands. It happened after one of my friends, Joy, attended a church gathering in Leicestershire; I didn't know she was going, and I had never heard of the medium. But during the evening she produced a painted portrait and asked if anyone recognised the face, and even asked if the name Maureen meant anything to anyone present. My friend immediately put up her hand and said: "That's the Maureen I know." I got a bit of a shock when the picture was forwarded on to me, because Joy didn't even put in an explanatory note. I didn't need one to realise who it was, indeed I was staggered at the accurate likeness of how I used to look (I must say that was a few years ago). I have never yet met the lady who drew the picture (signed in the name of Sandra), although I am still hoping to, even though I understand she has now left the Midlands. But she did pass on her blessing for me to reproduce the drawing – which is still among my treasured possessions – on any published work.

I also once had the experience of sitting in a room full of people watching a medium draw a picture of my father. She had never met me or my father, or even seen a photograph of him, but the likeness was uncanny. She didn't start in the orthodox artist's way with an outline, but instead pencilled in some features; when she emphasised the wrinkles on the forehead and added a tufty piece of hair, I knew instantly it was my dad.

I have since witnessed many such scenes where a picture has been drawn remotely and someone present will recognise the face.

Needless to say, I have tried a few drawings myself but not with any great success. And that's putting it mildly. "Get some bright colours and that will inspire you," I was told, but all I ended up with were a few swirls.

Unfortunately art was never one of my best subjects at school and every attempt I made ended up looking like one of LS Lowry's matchstick men, only not so good as his, obviously. In fact I still have a complex after my attempts were held up to ridicule in front of the whole class by the art mistress at school; it's funny how you never forget some things, and I've never forgotten her name, either. But as I now have to admit, we can't all be good at everything!

21 – Privileged to have The Gift

A ROCKING CHAIR

As I sit in my rocking chair
feeling free, peaceful and calm,
As I sit in the still and the quiet,
I reflect on where my life has gone.

I know I am on a new pathway of life,
one which will be free of bitterness and strife.
I know if I learn to look and listen,
God will show me the way as I struggle on from day to day.

God will give me an insight
on the right pathway to go.
I must learn to trust and have no doubt
because this is what life is all about.

People thank me in all sorts of ways after coming for a reading, many with gifts of flowers and plants – which I don't expect but nevertheless they are always well received. Presents with love always stop me in my tracks, and make me feel I have won the affection and respect of people who are feeling down and sometimes very sick. The fact that they take time out to send flowers can have a very sobering effect.

Flowers are my favourite gift and will always remind me of my father, as he loved his garden and his flower beds. The red roses were top of his list, so I'm afraid a bunch of those always brings a tear to me eye.

There were also a few sniffles after I received one of my favourite thank-you messages, which came from the spirit world and goes back to my school days. I suppose I inherited something of my mother's character in sticking up for the underdog, people I feel have been wronged; I know I stood up for one or two of my school friends when they were being picked on by the majority or by bullies, and it got me into the occasional fight. One girl – Anne, who was often taunted because she had one leg slightly shorter than the other and limped along – has since passed over and actually came through at one session to thank me. She must have lived quite a tortured life, but that message brought the memories flooding back from when we were good friends in our school days.

Now I am more embroiled in other people's relationships through the readings I give, and it does bring home to me the fact that there are very many unhappy people in this world. Many of the relationships I hear about are non-functional – I reckon about only one in ten can look me in the eye and say they are ecstatically happy – and I do hear some real horror stories. But I try and help through my knowledge of psychology, and if people leave in a better frame of mind than when they arrived, then I feel I have done my best to help the situation.

I have no idea how some people find me. They do say word of mouth is the best form of recommendation, and it must be because I have never advertised apart from a couple of lines in a local newspaper when I first moved house. It never ceases to amaze me how people from all walks of life do find me, and of course it is extremely encouraging and rewarding when they return ... some of them time after time. One recent call was from my very first client in the Swindon area – the doctor I mentioned in an earlier chapter; he said he was pleased to hear from one of his patients that I was still carrying out my good work in the locality, and I looked forward to seeing him again after seven years. When we met again, I am pleased to report, he seemed very satisfied and comforted by the messages I was able to pass on.

One of the best laughs I had was when a group of girls from London all piled into a car and found their way to my door. They were in a good mood when they arrived, and fortunately for me they were in an even happier frame of mind when they left for home.

I was put to the test many times in my early days as a medium, when I used to say to myself: "Hang on a minute, I don't want to do this." A fellow psychic once said to me: "Your pathway was no text-book route," and I had to agree. But I passed those tests, and I now know in my heart I will always be there for the spirit world and the spirits will always be there for me.

If I do come back in some future life, and I have a choice, I would choose to come back as my friend's cat – because he is spoiled rotten! I might have been spoiled as a youngster as the "baby" of the family to some extent, but I feel many of my lessons in life have been learned the hard way. And I am not blaming anyone – I'm big enough to own up and say in many instances I have been my own worst enemy. I was a glutton for punishment, but now I am more honest and willing to listen. I still have a sense of humour, albeit warped at times when I laugh in all the wrong places, but it keeps me alive and kicking. I won't give in, and feel I am a better person for embracing the spirits. I just hope my experience is an inspiration to others, and while I am sure many of today's young-sters will get drawn into spiritualism, they will unquestionably demand – and get – a much wider view of the world than we did in the last century. They will want more than being told they like ice-cream or fish and chips. They will want to see the proof and hear the truth.

When I say I now listen more, I mean I listen to my inner self rather than people preaching in churches. It is called listening to your own inner child, and it is a dormant gift that we all possess. My healing and counselling is offered through the spoken word; I am a firm believer in talking things through to let out the feelings of anger and guilt. Let's face it, they are emotions we all experience, but at the end of many sessions I have been warmly hugged by the people I have tried to help. "Thank you so much, I feel so much better for having spoken to you," they will say. How much more satisfac-tion does a medium or healer need? Sometimes all I have to do is be a good listener, to show the person who is hurting that there is someone at the end of the day who will care.

I believe it is one of God's universal laws that we learn a little lesson from everyone we meet in this life, and one of the most inspiring people I have come across is a lady who came to me suffering from ovarian cancer. Her positive attitude made me feel so humble – counselling her taught me a lot about tolerance, which I know was one of the factors a little lacking in my own make-up.

I now feel more buoyant because I am listening to what the powers that be are trying so hard to show me. "Make it easy on yourself" is my new philosophy on life, and the feedback I get from people is ten-fold compared to the days of depression. It's not always easy to do, but negative thoughts must be thrown out with the rubbish – that was one of the messages I received from my sister Pat after she passed away. Through this young medium Darren she told me: "Don't do anything you don't want to do." I knew full well what she meant – don't let people dump their baggage on me! I am fully aware that some people who visit me are more in need of a marriage guidance counsellor than a spiritualist, and after Pat's message I vowed to myself that I wouldn't keep taking repeat bookings from people like that. I am living proof that having a confident outlook has healing qualities in itself.

I know I don't have all the answers to the universe, but nevertheless I do try and keep an open mind when it comes to other people's ideas. The research goes on in medical and scientific fields, and still there are many questions unanswered.

I'm sure there are reasons behind every decision, we are just not aware of them. Take the latest economic recession – it hit a lot of families and individuals, but looking retrospectively at the situation it had to happen because the system was spiralling out of control. We have all purchased things that with hindsight we didn't really need, so maybe this was a way of making people take stock of their lives. I continue to be inspired by Mother Earth, and believe in the "no pain, no gain" proverb.

Looking around at the commercialisation of the world today, and the importance people place in materialism, it is easy to feel despondent. But I honestly feel many governments are now making strides and waking up to the frailties of the environment and our planet, which after all is needed for the survival of our children who represent all our tomorrows.

While out shopping on a winter's day I came upon a young street beggar who was talking to one of his acquaintances; he was full of smiles, definitely brightening up my day without realising it, while most of the passers-by had miserable faces that matched the weather. The incident made me stop in my tracks and think back to one of my father's philosophical sayings about life being like a stage; we each have our own pathway, our own learning curve.

I was on a roller-coaster ride in my earlier life and went into the wilderness for many years, carrying a feeling of bitterness, but that just chews you up, keeps you in a negative frame of mind and in fact makes you ill. Some parts of the journey were rough because I would not listen to the right people. Now I listen to my own intuition because I know this is the inner self. I no longer need people who think they know it all, and I don't suffer fools gladly. I have learned some lessons the hard way, but now I can think much clearer and am a better person for it. I am a living example that hope eventually leads towards the right pathway; I now have something to believe in and feel at one with the world.

Someone once told me to love myself and everything else will fall into place, and although I didn't believe it at the time, it is as if I have stepped off a train at a completely different junction. I now try my best to live life for the moment, because I know it is the greatest prize of all. But living in harmony with oneself is not a God-given right, it has to be worked for – sometimes against all the odds. It's a hard lesson of life, but you do have to learn to accept adversity and hit it head on. If the lessons I have learned inspire just one person who is lost, then I will consider this writing work of mine a worthwhile project.

Clients often turn up looking very stressed, but leave with a noticeable more relaxed look. This then is the power of loved ones in spirit; I am still amazed at how the spirit world connects its energies to our own, but having seen so many different aspects of this interaction to bring love and healing, I just appreciate the Gift I have been given and am not about to give up. I am so proud to have been chosen to help get across the message of eternal life. A good link-up still gives me a real buzz.

Life is an adventure, no matter how many bitter pills we have to swallow along the way – and I can put my hand on my heart and say I have swallowed more than my fair share. But I have come out of the rain into the sun; I have emerged from the tunnel a very different lady.

I know I inherited this spiritual Gift from my grandmother, but I was largely self-taught and so it was a bit of a hard slog, taking nearly half a life-time to polish. I also know another member of my family, a niece, has special psychic powers but at the moment her lifestyle moves around at 120 miles an hour. She is not what I call "grounded" and doesn't have the time to apply herself to the spiritual side. In fact she is more interested in the Tarot and Angel cards, which don't come anywhere near the top of my list.

I always knew my grand-daughter was gifted, from the things she would perceive and describe; I predicted when she was just three years old that she would one day become a medium, and she is still quite young, a teenager, which I think is too young to become involved. Mediumship can take over your life, so she has plenty of time ahead of her, but one day I will lend encouragement and help perpetuate this Gift in my family.

I now know that what I have is the most precious of all gifts, and that I have brought comfort and love to a lot of people. When I was younger I said to the spirit world: "Go away and leave me alone." I didn't ask for this to happen to me, but now I am older and wiser I can accept it and cherish my Gift because I know I am one of the chosen few. I never thought I would hear myself say this, but I do feel very privileged, and will continue to do the work of the spirits to the best of my ability.

TERRY WOODHOUSE has been a journalist for over 40 years, starting out on weekly newspapers in Suffolk and spending a couple of years in his early career on an English-language newspaper in North Africa. Since returning to England he has worked mostly as a sports journalist on regional evening newspapers, including the Oxford Mail and Swindon Evening Advertiser (a 17-year stint as sports editor), and over this period also contributed copy to every national newspaper and major TV channel.

For the last 16 years he has worked as a freelance, writing mainly for a business magazine but also acting as a PR consultant to various companies. He is still based in Wiltshire, although now has largely retired from the office to the golf course.